A Sense of Bel[...]

To Dave & Maggie

Hector Emmanuell

SIGNED ON 9th JULY 2016
@ BASKEYFIELD HOUSE
MIDDLEPORT
BURSLEM
S-O-T.

For my family and friends

A Sense of Belonging

*From the Rhondda to the Potteries:
Memories of a Welsh-Italian Englishman*

Hector Emanuelli

With illustrations by the author and photographs from his collection.

Six Towns Books

Copyright © 2010 Hector Emanuelli

All rights reserved. No part of this publication may be reproduced, stored in a retrieval system, or transmitted, in any form or by any means, electronic, mechanical, photocopying, recording or otherwise, without the prior consent of the copyright owner and the publisher.

Front cover:
Giovanni and Ettorino Emanuelli at
81 Bute Street Treorchy in 1922
Back cover:
Bardi and its castle in the 1920s.
Cover design:
Anthony Emanuelli

ISBN 978-1-4457-2947-3

First published in 2010 by
Six Towns Books
SixTownsBooks@aol.de

Foreword

I must confess that there have often been times during the many years of my now long life when I felt like an outsider. I spent my childhood in South Wales as the son of Italian immigrants. They ran a 'refreshment house' in Treorchy and as a young boy in the 1920s I sold confectionery from a tray in the Treherbert Opera House and at the Eisteddfod in Treorchy. I remember feeling very much like an Italian among the Welsh. Then, when I visited my parents' hometown in northern Italy at the tender age of seven with my OXO cup and Welsh accent, I felt like a little Welshman – *un piccolo gallese* – among Italians. Later still, as a teenager in the 1930s when the family moved to England my schoolmates made me feel like a Welshman among the English. The war years were worst: branded as being of 'hostile association' and detained in an internment camp on the Isle of Man, I had never felt so isolated in my life.

But now, after many years and among my many English friends, I am happy to see myself as what I am: a Welsh-Italian Englishman – e*d è buono così!* This is my story.

Hector Emanuelli, March 2010

Acknowledgements

Over the past few years I have written a body of texts in an attempt to retrieve some episodes of my life from the mists of the past. I am unsure what motivated me to do so, perhaps simply a desire to halt the march of time or preserve a dear memory from the oblivion of forgetfulness. But as the years passed by and the number of texts increased I began to think it would be worth the effort to combine them into a narrative or at least to make of them a cohesive whole reflecting some of the themes and preoccupations that have marked my life. The book your are now holding in your hands is the fruit of this effort. Its production proved to be a mammoth task and one that I should never have been able to discharge alone. Without the help of my friends and family, who have shown infinite patience answering a multitude of questions about things that occurred perhaps decades ago, it would never have come to fruition. I thank all these friends and members of my family for their help, but I should like to single out my brother Aldo for special thanks for the many hours he has been prepared to spend refreshing my memory of 'the old days,' looking at family photographs with me and putting 'names to faces.' Since I never learned to use word processors or computers, I have relied heavily on my son Anthony to turn my typewritten memories into a book. I should like to thank him for the many hours he has spent doing this. I also wish to thank his wife Margit for proof reading the book several times and for her many valuable suggestions on content and cover. I am also very grateful to my friend Hilary Baddeley for patiently going through what I have written with a toothcomb and weeding out many errors. My thanks also go to Matthew Sweet of the BBC for providing me with background information on some of my fellow detainees during World War II.

CONTENTS

Chapter 1   My Little Welsh Home   *1*

Chapter 2   Bardi Beckons   *13*

Chapter 3   Good-bye Rhondda   *29*

Chapter 4   A Shakespearean Interlude   *41*

Chapter 5   Catering for the Potters   *45*

Chapter 6   Mussolini: His Part in My Downfall *59*

Chapter 7   'Collar the Lot!'   *69*

Chapter 8   Castaway   *77*

Chapter 9   Directed Labour   *97*

Chapter 10 Building the Business   *109*

Chapter 11 Tying the Knot   *123*

Chapter 12 Luna di Miele   *133*

Chapter 13 A Booming Business   *147*

Chapter 14 The Great Meltdown   *161*

Chapter 15 The Happy Years   *169*

Chapter 16 Epilogue   *183*

CHAPTER 1

My Little Welsh Home

'Years and years ago, when I was a boy, when there were wolves in Wales, and birds the colour of red-flannel petticoats whisked past the harp-shaped hills,...'
Dylan Thomas, A Child's Christmas in Wales

The fog of over eighty years lifts briefly. It is 1927, I am seven years old and the weather is wintry. I am on my way home from school. I am standing spellbound before the front-room window of a terraced house. Behind the window, a brightly-coloured and glossy-surfaced oil painting is prominently displayed on an easel. Illuminated in warm electric light, its glowing colours and the shiny, glossy surface of the paint fascinate me! At my side, my younger brother Luigino stands patiently with our faithful dog Bob. Minutes pass. Luigino is tugging at my sleeve: 'Come on Ettorino. We're late. Ma will be worried!'

The spell is broken, but as I turn away from the window I resolve to try and copy that wonderfully glossy effect as soon as I get home.

'Home' was a few rooms behind and above a 'refreshment house' in Bute Street, Treorchy, a mining town in the Rhondda valley. The painting I had been admiring was my daily treat on the way to and from school in nearby Penyrenglyn. Perhaps it was the work of a hobby painter, possibly a miner working in one of the local collieries. The painting would be changed every now and then. I would stop for several minutes each day to admire whatever picture was on display. I always loved the colours. But what fascinated me most was the shiny, glossy surface of the painting. Even at this tender age I adored playing around with my standard school-issue of water colour paints. On dark winter evenings and in a world without television and other distractions I could spend hours at the kitchen table sloshing about with my water colours, turning out smeary pictures of whole menageries of pretty much indistinguishable dogs and cats, horses and cows. Elephants, camels and zebras were easier on account of long noses, long necks and stripes, respectively. My use of colour was generous! But the final results were somehow disappointing. Everything was drab and matt compared to what I saw behind that window. How could I possibly achieve that glossy finish? The embryo of an idea began to form in my young mind!

Luigino, Bob and I were home in a few minutes. My father stood smoking a *sigaro toscano* on the step of the refreshment house he ran with my mother. Above the shop front a sign proclaimed in fine gold lettering 'Pure Ices – G. EMANUELLI – Confectionery.'

My father looked as tired as his sign. He'd come to a booming South Wales from the small hill-town of Bardi in northern Italy back in 1905. He'd been in Wales ever since, apart from brief spells back home in 1918 when he drove a Fiat 18 b truck for the Italian army during the Great War. It was after he had been discharged in 1919 that he married my mother.

When he finally returned to Wales with my mother-to-be in late 1919 he found the coal boom that had attracted him and his fellow Italians to Wales was over and business was slackening off. As the downturn escalated into depression, people were starting to move out of South Wales and my father's profits were contracting with the population.

Now, fatigued from a long day of making ice-cream, serving in the refreshment house and turning a meagre profit, he cast us a severe glance, pulling out the fob-watch from his waistcoat pocket with a meaningful look.

I pushed open the frosted-glass shop door, and Luigino, Bob and I trotted in. Ma was behind the mahogany confectionery counter. The wall behind her was lined with shelves heavy with bottles containing various colourful cordials, ginger beers and 'pop'. This was a 'temperance bar' and there was not a drop of alcohol for sale. Below the cordials and pop, large glass jars held multi-coloured sweets and toffees. The 'pièce de résistance' was a mock-marble soda fountain sporting two splendid brass taps for making soft drinks. Apart from the proprietors, there was nothing Italian about our refreshment house. The 'product range' was purely British. Beverages consisted of mugs of hot Bovril, Oxo and tea. Coffee was virtually unheard of until the 1930s. British trade names from the confectionery and tobacco industries, such as Fry's, Cadbury's and Rowntree's chocolates, Wills's Gold Flake and Player's Navy Cut cigarettes with their colourful packing took pride of place. Everything was a long way away from the scents and fragrances of a refined Italian 'bar.' But one thing that the refreshment house did provide was a place for the young miners to gather to talk and play dominoes, all day, every day, even Sundays.

'*Dove siete stati*? Where've you been?' asked Ma reproachfully, peering down from above the mahogany counter and the brass rail that ran along its front. Without answering, we made a beeline for the room at the back of the shop.

The young miners sitting at a table playing a noisy game of dominoes and sipping cups of hot OXO greeted us more cordially as we passed. 'Watch this,' shouted one of them. Pulling back his elbows and sticking out his neck, he launched a well-aimed globule of spit that described a graceful arc spanning a couple of yards to land with a satisfying splat and a hiss on the black, cast-iron pot-bellied stove that heated the room.

Spitting at the stove was a much-loved winter sport for the young miners. Hits were rewarded with applause. Misses were absorbed by the sawdust strewn on the floor. All the same, for obvious reasons of hygiene my father disapproved strongly of this pastime. '*Porca miseria!*' he would shout, 'don'ta spit on de stove, boys. 'Ow often I 'av' to tell you?' This would elicit from the culprit a contrite, though insincere, 'Sorry John'. My father's real name, of course, was Giovanni, but everyone in Wales simply called him John.

At the back of the shop a door opened onto the building's 'private quarters.' I headed straight for the kitchen, keen to try out my idea of how to get that nice glossy finish on my pictures. I must have heard about 'oil painting' somewhere for the brilliant solution I had lit upon was a readily obtainable commodity: olive oil!

This might seem odd for a child in a South Wales mining town at a time long before the 'Mediterranean Diet' had became a European-wide fad and when olive oil was a scarcity in British homes, but in the seven or so years she had been in Wales my mother had remained true to her culinary roots. So olive oil was a staple in our household. It was not hard to requisition a supply of it from the pantry – and I was soon mixing it merrily with my water colours in the hope of recreating that *miner's high gloss*.

The results were disappointing, not to say catastrophic! What was supposed to be a high-sheen finish was simply a greasy mess. Olive oil seemed to be everywhere! Fortunately, perhaps, the fog of forgetfulness closes in again at this point. I can no longer recall and can only imagine my mother's reaction to what I had done to her kitchen table!

Apart from these first faltering steps in the art of oil painting, I also remember some of my early attempts at handwriting. Not surprisingly, these took place at the Boys' Junior School just down the road in Penyrenglyn, which translates charmingly into English as 'Home of the Angel.'

Before we started a handwriting exercise, I recall that our teacher, the tall, slender, frail and gentle Miss Hopkins, would insist we write the date at the top of each page. I still have a sheet from one of my school books. The date is 12.4.1927. What puzzled me, I remember, was that the first two numbers changed pretty often, but the last one – 1927 – seemed as if it would never change. A complete mystery to me at that time.

My handwriting was rather neat and tidy. Later, as a youth, I developed an interest in 'lettering' and dreamt of becoming a 'graphic artist.' Perhaps this later interest was inspired in me by my Welsh teacher, as my interest in painting had been by the Welsh miner! The handwriting exercise on the surviving sheet is written in Welsh. It consists of a list of Welsh words the meaning of which I have now forgotten, though I can still hear Miss Hopkins reading them out to us from the blackboard with her musical Welsh voice: 'briallu,' 'blodau,' 'melyn' (after consulting a Welsh-English dictionary I can now identify these as primrose, flower, yellow).

My mind must have been a linguistic Tower of Babel. Many of the miners who patronised my father's refreshment house spoke Welsh, as did many of my classmates at school. My parents spoke their local Italian dialect to each other at home, but curiously they would switch to standard Italian – 'il vero italiano' – when fellow Italians from their home town came to visit. With the other children Luigino and I spoke English, and at school the teachers were obviously keen to drum some Welsh into our young minds, all of which, unfortunately, I have forgotten, although I can still give a pretty convincing rendering of tongue-twisting Welsh place-names such as Ystradyfodwg, Llwynypia and Tynewydd.

All this linguistic confusion may have been one of the reasons for the stutter I suffered from when I was a young boy. I had great difficulty getting out the words and preferred to say nothing when possible.

My great dread was for the errands my mother was wont to send me out on. Always busy in the 'shop,' she relied on Luigino and me to get things for her. 'Ettorino, mi fanno male *i piedi* – my feet are tired, go to Davies the chemist and get me some *Zam-Buk* ointment!' The very idea of trying to pronounce the name of this product inspired fear in me. I could already hear myself stuttering out 'Za-Za-Za-Zam-Boo-Boo-Book.' But off I went to the chemist's, rehearsing *'a jar of Zam-Buk ointment please, a jar of Zam-Buk ointment please'* over and over in my head. When I got to the chemist's, I looked through the window and saw customers waiting to be served. I knew I should never be able to get those words out. I turned on my heel and returned home. When my mother asked where the ointment was, I replied 'Se-se-se-sold out!' The first conscious lie!

There were other errands that I found less challenging. One errand that I was often sent on after the end of the school day was to Lipton's grocers. My mission here was to procure 'cracked eggs' for my father's ice-cream production. For some reason I found it easier to say 'cracked eggs' than 'Zam-Buk ointment.' Another regular errand took me across the road to the communal bake-house, where I would have my mother's apple-pies baked for a penny. But this required few linguistic skills and I accomplished my mission with ease.

By around 1927 my father had set up a second shop in addition to the one he had opened at 81 Bute Street in Treorchy in 1921. The new shop was in Treherbert, confusingly also in Bute Street, but this time at number 138. It was about a mile and half from the shop in Treorchy, which my father entrusted to a manager, a gentle Irishman by the name of Arthur Delanty. Although virtually identical with the refreshment house in Treorchy, the Treherbert shop offered more living space and was quieter located in a quieter spot. The river, the Rhondda Fawr, oozed black and oily down the valley at the bottom of our garden, and we could see the bare hills climbing behind it. Kelly's 1926 Trade Directory describes Treherbert as follows: 'The town lies amongst mountainous and picturesque scenery at the foot of Penpych, which rises 1,700 feet above the level of the sea; it is 11 miles north-west from Pontypridd.'

Strangely, I have little or no recollection of this 'mountainous and picturesque scenery.' My parents were always busy with their shop, day in, day out, and Luigino and I were either at school or helping with the 'business.' There were no walks in the countryside, no visits to places of interest, no Sunday afternoon strolls, no summer picnics, no sports with the local boys. No visits to befriended families. Our horizons were largely limited to a few streets in Treherbert and Treorchy. And my family was hardly an exception here. Invariably, the Italians running shops in the Rhondda would open their doors at six in the morning, only to close them as late as possible in the evening. Eleven o'clock was not unusual. The margins that could be made on ice-creams, soft-drinks, chocolates and cigarettes were wafer thin and every penny counted.

The one big exception to this endless round of labour came just once a year. The annual charabanc outing! Every summer the Bracchis, Rabaiottis, Gazzis, Fulgonis, Carpaninis, Contis, Sidolis, Assiratis, Bacchettas, Bernis, Contis, Cordanis, Zanellis, Feccis, Carinis, Lusardis, Mascherpas, Moruzzis, Resteghinis, Rissis, Riccis, Rossis, Salvanellis, Cordanis, Servinis, Franchis, Solaris, Sterlinis, Strinatis, Tedaldis, Zeraschis and, yes, even the Emanuellis would sign a truce to shut their shops, hire a charabanc or two and head off on a day trip to a not-too-distant resort. This was a great event and was no doubt one of the few where the people of Bardi, the Bardigiani, came together as a community. Of course, there was always the odd 'black leg' who would break the truce, stay at home and keep his shop open in a shoddy attempt to profit from the temporary absence of competition. But this was universally frowned upon.

I remember such charabanc outings with particular pleasure as they gave me an opportunity to see the girl who was to become my 'childhood sweetheart.' The lovely Alma Carpanini! Alma was the eldest of the three daughters of Angelo and Maria Carpanini. My mother and Maria had grown up together in Bardi. Like my father, Angelo had emigrated from Bardi to South Wales and together with his wife had set up in business in Aberdare, opening a fish and chip restaurant. This proved to be very successful and was known among the miners and their families as 'Carps.' Angelo, or Angie as with familiarity we had learnt to call him, had the third finger of his left hand missing. Luigino and I often wondered about this and discussed it often. Had he lost his finger whilst cutting his chips? Angie would never confirm or deny this. So we never knew!

Angelo was also the proud owner of a motor cycle and sidecar. He would occasionally venture out on the New Road across the mountain that separated Aberdare from the Rhondda to visit my parents. He always brought his daughter Alma with him. I took to her instantly despite the faint scent of fried fish that followed her everywhere!

Surprisingly, however, my parents' best friends were not fellow Italians, but Wilhelmina and Tom James. Tom worked in the cooperative butcher's shop in Treorchy. My father and he would spend hours chatting in the evenings, either at the Conservative Club or in my parents' refreshment bar. Tom James loved everything that was new in the world of technology and introduced my father to the delights of thermionic valves, cat's whiskers and the radio, which was then at the cutting edge of technology. Wilhelmina was my mother's very best friend. In fact, one might call her my mother's Welsh sister. It was Wilhelmina who taught her English and tutored her in it with indefatigable patience.

Wilhelmina and Tom had a daughter called Netta and a son called Walter. My brother and I often played with Walter. He had a Meccano set. So did I, but his set was superior, with cog wheels and clockwork motors. He obviously benefited from his father's love of all things technical. I was very envious! His sister, Netta, who called me 'Etto' and took me to the pictures to see my first cowboy films, was as close as a sister to me. Indeed, if we had any sense of belonging back in those early days in the Rhondda it was undoubtedly thanks to the James family.

My early attempts at writing in April 1927. Everything is in Welsh and I was called Ettorino at the time.

Penyrenglyn Junior Boys School. That's me, second row, third from the right. Miss Hopkins is at the back of the room.

My father Giovanni Emanuelli and my mother Carolina Tedaldi in the early 1920s.

Mother and father in the Treorchy shop. Note the mock-marble soda fountain.

My father and I outside the shop at 81 Bute Street Treorchy in the early 1920s.

A general view of Treorchy, where my parents ran their first refreshment house and temperance bar in the 1920s and early 1930s.

Myself and my brother when we were still called Ettorino and Luigino.

CHAPTER 2

Bardi Beckons

> *'poi giunsi in una valle inculta e fiera,*
> *di ripe cinta e spaventose tane,*
> *che nel mezzo s' un sasso avea un castello*
> *forte e ben posto, a maraviglia bello.'*[*]
> Ludovico Ariosto, Orlando Furioso, Canto II St. 41

My young mind was full of Bardi before I had ever seen it. My mother and father were always talking about it. I had heard the names of its surrounding villages and hamlets a hundred times. My mother's birth place, Barsia di Sotto, recurred often, but they also talked of Grezzo, Carpana, Credarola, Stradella, Cereseto, Corti di Sopra, Compiano, Borgotaro, Bedonia and many, many more. Bardi had taken on a magic aura for me, becoming a fairy-tale land where ghosts haunted the medieval castle, goblins and sprites played mischievous tricks in its woods, knights in armour battled with dragons and pilgrims took respite on their wearisome way from Canterbury to Rome.

    My mother told me that a magnificent river flowed past the little farmstead where she had been born. She called it the Ceno and said it was twenty times bigger than the Rhondda

---

[*] Then a wild, untamed vale I came upon,
Encircled by steep slopes and awesome lairs,
Where atop a rock loomed a castle bold,
Well placed and most beautiful to behold.

and that I would be able to catch fish in its clean and sparkling water. In hushed tones she told me of Soleste and Moroello, two lovers who had died a tragic death a thousand years ago and whose souls still haunted the castle in Bardi. She also told me I should be wary of the 'folletti' or bad fairies who would try to lure me into the woods with promises of treasure to be found in magic lakes.

By 1927, after some seven and a half years of unrelenting toil in the Rhondda my mother was beginning to feel the strain. She needed a break and was missing her family back in Bardi. So when school broke up for the holidays it was decided she would go back home to spend the summer in Barsia di Sotto, where she had lived as a girl.
And I was to go with her!

I couldn't wait to get there! All the same, I was a little apprehensive and I remember quite clearly that I insisted on taking with me – for my protection – not my teddy bear, but my OXO cup! This cup was my childhood fetish and talisman and under no circumstances would I drink out of anything else. I never left home without it and it even accompanied me to Sunday school. And I reckoned that in Bardi I could do with a shield against the elves and gnomes that I would undoubtedly encounter there!

I do not have much recollection of the journey from Treorchy across the Channel through France and Switzerland into Italy, but it must have been quite an ordeal for my mother with a seven-year-old in tow, not to mention all the luggage needed for a lengthy stay in Bardi. But I do recall the final stage of the journey as the Fiat 'corriera' that carried us from Parma's 'Stazione Centrale' turned the final bend in the valley and Bardi and its castle loomed into view. It was love at first sight! A love that was to last all my life. The 'castello' rose majestically from the evening mist that shrouded the 'antico borgo' huddled in its shadow and the river snaked away in a silver line to a pale blue horizon. This really was the fairyland my mother had told me so much about, I thought.

As we disembarked in the dusty Piazza del Mercato, I cast a glance over my shoulder at the haunted castle, looming large over the town, and scanned the square for any sign of the 'folletti.' All clear, I thought. But I was still glad that I'd brought my OXO mug!

My grandfather Giovanni Tedaldi was waiting for us in the square. He was a strong-looking man in his late forties, wearing a black broad-rimmed hat, a black waistcoat, a black jacket and black trousers. In fact everything he wore was black, except his dazzlingly white shirt, which he wore buttoned up at the neck, but without a tie. I noticed his boots were very muddy. I would never have been allowed to go out like that, I thought! I glanced around and saw that all the other men in the square were dressed identically. And their boots were just as muddy. He picked me up, shook me enthusiastically and exclaimed 'Benvenuto Ettorino!'

After some conversation and many hugs and kisses between the adults, we headed off for Barsia di Sotto down by the river. We took a winding track down to the farmstead. At times it was stony, at times muddy, and my boots were soon in the same shape as my grandfather's. At home in Treorchy, my mother would not have been pleased. But here she did not seem to notice. 'This is a good place for a boy to be,' I thought. Mother explained that this path was the one that she had taken every day on her way to work as a waitress at the Bue Rosso Hotel when she was a girl. As we reached the end of the path the farmhouse came into view with the mountain of Pizzo D'Oca with its slopes coming down to the river Ceno in the background, and my mother broke out in tears.

In front of the farmhouse was a hayrick, I had never seen a hayrick before, there was a group of children playing around it in the evening light. They appeared to be chasing rabbits. This naturally captured my attention, I abandoned my mother and ran towards them. 'Now if you make a hole in this hayrick the rabbits would burrow there and would be safe,' I said. Of course they did not understand a word I had said, although magically I could understand everything they said to me. A week later I was conversing with them in the local Bardigiano – or as they called it – the Bardesan dialect. And just as magically, I was no longer stuttering!

These were indeed happy days at Barsia di Sotto, what a contrast to the dark, coal-blackened, bare valleys of the Rhondda. The sun seemed to be always shining and I soon became accustomed to life on the farm.

One day my cousin Pierino, one of the sons of my mother's brother Antonio, took me fishing on the banks of the River Ceno. We made our way from his father's house above the village down the paths to the Ceno at the bottom of the valley. 'The river rises below Monte Penna,' he told me, 'and rushes down to the town of Fornovo, where it changes its name to Taro, and then flows on to join the great river Po that flows to the sea.' 'Where I live,' I said, 'we have the Rhondda Fawr. It trickles down the valley behind our house until it gets to Porth, where it changes its name to the Taff.' 'The Ceno,' Pierino continued, 'changes its name, too. It is a fine and honest river, he continued, but a sleepy one. It has a brother over the hill called Taro. He is a fine river, too, but less honourable. One day, long ago, these two brothers, Ceno and Taro, decided to organize a race to see who could get to Fornovo the fastest. Whoever got there first would have the honour of giving his name to the river that runs from Fornovo to the Po. They agreed to start the following night as soon as the moon rose. Ceno fell asleep immediately, dreaming of the long journey ahead. But Taro waited and as soon as he was certain that his brother Ceno was sleeping he threw himself headlong into the valley, rushing precipitously down through the rocky valley. The moon was already high in the sky when Ceno awoke with a yawn. Looking left and right for his brother Taro to start the race, Ceno was surprised and disappointed to see that Taro had tricked him. All the same, he threw himself into the valley in a desperate attempt to catch up with his rascal of a brother, but all his efforts were in vain and by the time he arrived at Fornovo his brother Taro had already passed the town and was well on his way to join the Po. From that day onwards the river from Fornovo to the Po has been called Taro and the Ceno ends at Fornovo.'

Ending his story and admonishing me never to trust anyone from the neighbouring Val di Taro, Pierino discarded his boots and socks and waded into brother Ceno. I followed suit. It appeared that the fish, I do not recall if they were carp or trout, would shelter beneath projecting rocks or boulders. The trick was to hit the sheltering rock with a heavy stone, so stunning the fish. All wholesome food is caught without a net or a trap! And the trick worked! Not only did we bring home a good catch for dinner that evening, for which we were heartily praised, but we also had great fun splashing about in the river.

It was a very hot sunny afternoon and I was idly playing in one of the meadows close to the farm when I suddenly saw these marvellous – or so I thought – creatures. They were multi-coloured and they fascinated me. I had never seen these in Treorchy. They were, of course, grasshoppers. I felt that I must take these back home to show Zia Anna. With some effort I was eventually able to capture a handful of these beauties, which I stuffed into my pockets, and made my way to the farmhouse. 'Guarda Zia! Look Auntie!' I exclaimed. 'Look what I have brought you.' I emptied the contents of my pockets onto Zia Anna's freshly scrubbed-kitchen table. True to their name, my treasures hopped all over the place, into the cooking pots, the flour bin, and with shrieks of anger and flying skirts Zia Anna chased me out of the kitchen. I took refuge in the orchard and consoled myself by gorging on peaches and figs. I was eventually forgiven of course, but even today just mention the word grasshopper and a smile comes to my face.

My mother's brother, Zio Toni, took me on several of his occasional hunting trips up into the mountains, showing me the secret places to which he would return in October to gather the finest 'funghi porcini' mushrooms that were to be found in the region. The true 'fungaiolo,' he said, was jealous of 'i suoi posti' – his favourite places – and so I should be honoured he was showing me his, and raising a finger to his lips he urged discretion on me with a conspiratorial 'zitto, zitto!', scanning the woods from right to left.

He would point out trees whose branches had a distinctive configuration. 'I'm keeping my eye on that!' he would say. 'Those branches are just right for making runners for the sledges.' Sledges were still used on the farm for transporting goods. Pulled by a pair of oxen they were more efficient than wheeled carts, especially along the stony hill paths. Other branches, he explained, were ideal for fashioning into yokes for the oxen. These were jobs for the dark winter nights when he would carve intricate patterns on these yokes and collars. I do not know if the oxen appreciated this artistic touch.

We climbed high into the woods, where the charcoal burners lived. Here we lingered, taking our repast with a chunk of home-baked bread, a bunch of grapes and farmhouse cheese with, of course, the customary flask of wine. We visited remote farmsteads where we were always made welcome and where Zio Toni would stay and exchange news and gossip.

Later in life, I learned that at the end of the last war many escaped British airmen were to seek refuge in these isolated farms. The local farmers would feed, house and hide them at considerable risk as German and fascist troops combed the mountains for escapees.

Whilst passing through little isolated villages we would meet other relatives. We would be detained while family gossip and a glass or two of wine were exchanged. Of course, I would produce my OXO cup, much to everyone's amazement.

Zio Toni bagged a couple of rabbits on one of our hunting trips. He was a good shot. He told me that it was important to be a good shot because cartridges were very expensive in Bardi. We had our picnic lunch. I loved to watch him expertly carve a hunk of bread with his clasp knife from the hard crusty loaf, a lump of home-made cheese, some grapes and a swig of ruby-red gutturnio from the neighbouring colli piacentini, and for me water from the nearby spring, of course from my OXO cup, and we were well satisfied.

Making our way back home we stopped and passed the time of day with the charcoal burners, the 'carbonari,' who still operated in those parts of the woods. They were a jolly lot with their blackened faces and pearly white teeth! They reminded me of the Rhondda miners stopping by in our shop for a mug of hot Bovril on their way home from work. My uncle told me the carbonari spent most of their life up in the mountains.

By this time I was getting quite hungry again and I was looking forward to our evening meal. 'Stasera mangiamo una bella polenta concia con ragù di coniglio' – this evening we shall have a nice plate of polenta with rabbit sauce – said Zio Toni, holding up his rabbits. I was sure that there would be one of Zia Anna's 'torte di frutta'. Or perhaps she would make another 'castagnaccio,' a delicious local pie made of chestnut flour, and sprinkled with pine nuts. Zia Anna was an excellent pastry cook and her fruit flans and tarts were out of this world. Obviously she had the advantage of fresh eggs and fruit from the farm, but even so all the cooking was done in an outdoor wood-burning oven and it must have taken great skill to regulate temperatures and times. Mind you, at seven years of age, I knew nothing about these matters. Incidentally, I remember being impressed by the fact that the wood ash from the ovens was saved and used to wash clothes. Nothing went to waste. I can recall that nearly all necessities were produced on the farm. We were virtually self-sufficient. Milk, cream, butter, cheese were all produced. Flour from wheat and chestnuts were stored in a large chest in the farmhouse. Pasta was made as and when required. Vegetables of every description grew in the kitchen-garden together with all kinds of herbs. There was every variety of fruit, figs, cherries, pears, apples and peaches. Salami was produced from the pigs, and there was of course home-grown wine, and one of its bi-products, vinegar. Looking back I believe the only things that were bought at the market on Thursdays were olive oil and coffee beans and, of course, the mezzo toscano cigars for Nonno Giovanni. If I was lucky I got a few caramelle, but not always.

My grandfather's farm was not very big and during the few months we stayed I soon got used to the routine and the animals. Ploughing was done with a pair of beautiful cream-coloured oxen. They were called Moro and Toro, and I became very fond of them. Although they were very slow, they were also very placid and patient. I loved to go ploughing with uncle and the oxen. He would urge them with 'va su Moro, va su Toro!' They usually took no notice. They even allowed me to ride on their backs. There were also chickens, pigs and a horse named Pina.

Uncle would often complain that the farmers down on the plain had it easy and did not appreciate their good luck in having such good soil to work with whereas in the hills around Bardi the soil was of poor quality and did not yield much. 'Loda il monte e tienti al piano,' he would mutter under his breath – 'Praise the hills, but keep to the plains,' the highlander's eternal lament.

Thursday was market day in Bardi and the following day being Thursday plans were afoot for a day out. My grandfather and my uncle would be attending the cattle market. Arrangements were made for me to be accompanied to Bardi by my cousins Gina and Maria, the daughters of my father's half-sister, Domenica, who were staying with us in my honour. Zia Anna told me I should also be able to meet Zio Pain' at the market. He was the widower of my mother's elder sister Beatrice, who had died just two years earlier, too young, at the age of forty-two.

My mother explained that I hadn't met Zio Pain' yet as he spent most of his time on the road travelling around the region, for he was a painter and decorator and it took him a year to complete his round. Almost all of the farmhouses had whitewashed walls and ceilings, she explained, and he was an expert in decorating these with friezes of flowers and garlands of foliage. The local parish priests would also commission him to redecorate or touch up the many roadside shrines that are to be found in and around the villages. I was keen to meet him. Perhaps, I thought, he could teach me how to get that fine miner's gloss!

The walk from the farm to Bardi took us along the rough and stony path that led steeply uphill in the shadow of the castle, and it was not until we were within a very short distance of the town that I learnt of another local custom: suddenly, my two female cousins left my side and disappeared giggling behind the hedge. There they removed their heavy everyday boots and skirts and reappeared in their best shoes and dresses. The exchange of clothing would be repeated on the journey home. My cousins had no intention of being outclassed by their town friends.

All the villagers from around Bardi were there, it seemed, the men making for the cattle market to buy and sell livestock. In Piazza del Mercato there were animals everywhere: to the right the oxen, to the left the cows with their calves. The pigs grunted in front of the Bue Rosso. Horses, sheep, mules and donkeys were traded behind the Chiesa di San Giovanni Battista, just off the Piazza del Mercato. The men were engaged in what seemed to me endless and furious arguments, shouting at the top of their voices. They were, of course, simply negotiating a fair price. Children dashed among the cows. Keeping a careful eye on their proprietors, they would wait until they were distracted by their violent negotiations before extracting an improvised container in which to catch the milk they had hastily extracted from the patient cows' udders. They drank this 'buon latte fresco' rapidly, disappearing before the cattle owner had sealed the sale with a handshake and could dedicate his full attention again to the herd.

My mother, Zia Anna and we children toured the various market stalls where we bought *caramelle* and – what seemed very strange to me – necklaces made of hazel nuts. The nuts were, of course, still in their shells. Whenever we wanted to eat one we would simply crack the shell and pull the nut off the necklace.

As promised, Zio Pain' was indeed at the market. He wore the usual broad-brimmed hat, but pulled down at the front over his twinkling, mischievous eyes, and tilted slightly, lending him a rather nonchalant look. Unlike so many others he was also wearing a tie, the dignity of which was somewhat diminished by the splashes of paint and colour on his jacket and trousers. But his boots, I remember, were not muddy!

My mother had obviously told him of my olive-oil painting escapade in her kitchen in Treorchy and his greeting was to pat me on the head saying, 'noi artisti, dobbiamo stare uniti! – we artists should stick together.' He promised to take me with him on his next commission and show me how he mixed his colours. 'When?' I asked eagerly. 'Domani, domani' he answered, adroitly removing a nut from my walnut necklace and waving as he disappeared into the market crowd.

As the market square emptied and the men retired to the Bue Rosso for refreshment, we too headed home down the hill to Barsia di Sotto. The end of another fine Bardigiano day.

The next morning, as appointed, Zio Pain' was waiting in front of the farmstead with his cart laden with buckets, ladders and brushes. He hoisted me up beside him with a hearty 'Buongiorno Ettorino, andiamo!' and off we set at a trot as his donkey moved off up the hill.

'We are going to Cereseto,' he said. From then on he didn't stop talking. He told me how Bardi had got its name. 'A long time ago in Roman times a general called Hannibal came over the Alps with his army to attack Rome, his arch enemy. With him he brought elephants, which terrified the Romans and brought him many a victory. But after many years the tide of fortune turned and he was forced to retreat back across the Alps. On the way he passed through the Val di Ceno with his army and his one remaining elephant, Bardus. The locals found the elephant terrifying, but the children found him friendly and even playful and asked if they could keep him. No longer needing the animal, Hannibal agreed. So Bardus remained here for the rest of his life and when he died a hundred years later, the locals renamed the town after him!'

I asked him if he had heard the story of Moroello and Soleste, the ghosts that my mother mentioned in whispered tones on our arrival. 'Sì, sì, te lo racconto – yes, yes, I'll tell you it,' and he launched enthusiastically into the tale. 'Soleste lived long ago in the days when the Landi Princes ruled Bardi. She was the young and fair daughter of the lord of the castle. She had fallen in love with the handsome captain Moroello, the commander of the castle's garrison. One day, he sallied out at the head of his troops to defend the town against marauding enemies who were devastating the valleys of the Ceno and Noveglia. He was gone many weeks and every day Soleste would climb the castle's highest tower and scan the horizon for signs of his return. One day she saw soldiers descending the valley of the river Noveglia, which joins the Ceno at the foot of the castle. When the troops reached the confluence of the two rivers she saw that they were not wearing the Landi colours, and in the certainty that Moroello had perished in battle she threw herself down to her death from the castle-keep. But Moroello had not perished, he had won a great victory and his troops had merely donned the colours of their defeated enemies as a sign of their triumph. When Moroello heard of the death of Soleste he too jumped to his death from the battlements of Piazza d'Armi and since then his tormented soul has haunted the keep of the castle.'

With these and other stories to while away the time, we wound our way up the serpentine road that climbed southwards out of Bardi up the hill through the woods of oak, chestnut, pine and beech towards Cereseto. You can imagine how spellbound I was by these and other fantastic tales told to the rhythm of the donkey's hooves as it plodded along the road with no other sound than birdsong and the breeze in the tree tops! We disembarked in front of the parish church in the sleepy hamlet of Cereseto. We were surrounded by barking –

though harmless – dogs who seemed pleased at the novelty of visitors. Opposite the church stood the baptistery. The door stood open and inside we could see workmen undertaking repairs to the ancient building. The interior was elaborately painted, but was much in need of restoration. After greeting his fellow workmen, Zio Pain' unloaded his cart and set about his work, mixing powders with pigments of burnt sienna and ochre, and one that I found particularly attractive, a glorious ultramarine blue. He allowed me to help him by stirring this blue in a bucket. I was delighted to be helping and I can see that wonderful blue to this day. He told me he usually used this ultramarine for the ceilings of shrines and when it was dry he would embellish it with gold stars. The interior walls of the baptistery were bare, but above the white cornice that topped them everything was painted. Climbing his ladder, Zio Pain' chatted away as he started work on intricate geometric and floral decorations in gold, blue and red. He added some touches of restorative colour to one of the trompe-l'œil windows painted in the lunettes above the cornice. I was enthralled by the finished work.

As he worked away Zio Pain' asked if I knew that this village was where my grandfather came from. He had been born here, he told me, before he married and went to live in Bardi and then in Paris. Perhaps he had even been baptised here, who knows? He chatted on and on until it was time to pack up his tools and materials and go home.

The ride back down the hill in the evening light was even more enchanting than the trip up the hill. Bardi Castle glowed in the warm sunlight and the river behind it shone like molten gold as it meandered away to the horizon.

Finally, we pulled up in front of the farmstead in Barsia di Sotto. The castle and the old town of Bardi already cast a deep shadow over it. My mother came out smiling to greet us and as she held out her arms to help me down I said earnestly 'Mother, I want to be a painter!'

Our holiday was drawing to a close and I felt a distinctive sadness in the air. Mother and Zia Anna were making plans to pay final visits to friends and relatives. They visited old girlhood friends and distant relatives in the most remote hamlets. There were of course hugs, tears and kisses as my mother said her sad farewells, and I too was very melancholy to realise I would soon be leaving this enchanting place where I had experienced so much love, affection and such glorious fun with my Italian uncles and cousins. I was not looking forward to it at all.

The final visit over, we slowly made our way back to the farm for the last time. It was a lovely evening, a rosy glow in the sky. In the distance the bell from the parish church tolled its call for evening benediction. From across the valley came the sound of a group of contadini singing one of those haunting mountain songs. They had brought in the grape harvest and were celebrating. As we approached the farm, cattle were being brought in for the night. Grandfather met us on the threshold. He was smoking his last mezzo toscano before going in and working a while on his yoke before the light gave out. Zia Anna had already made a start on packing the suitcases. I went into the stable and said goodbye to the soft-eyed oxen Moro and Toro and Pina the horse.

Little did I know it, and I would have been horrified if I had, but it was to be another twelve years before I was to set foot in Bardi again, and my second visit was to take place under far less auspicious circumstances.

The next day as we boarded the corriera in the Piazza del Mercato I thought 'I do hope Zia Anna has not forgotten to pack my OXO cup!'

The main street in Bardi. My father sent this postcard from Bardi to Treorchy in 1926.

My cousins Gina and Maria. That's me in the middle. All dressed up for the photographer. Bardi 1927.

Bardi Castle watching over the confluence of the Ceno and the Noveglia.

My mother's home at Barsia di Sotto. How I loved it!

CHAPTER 3

Good-bye Rhondda

*'Farewell the colliery worker, the muffler and the cap
Farewell you Rhondda Valley girls, we never will come back
The mines they are a-closing, the valleys all are doomed
There's no work in the Rhondda boys, we'll be in London soon.'
Frank Hennessy, Farewell to the Rhondda*

I cannot recall our return to the Rhondda. I can only assume that the contrast between my enchanted summer in the Apennines and the humdrum of everyday life in industrial South Wales was a bleak one for a young boy, bleak enough for Bardi to take on the role of a paradise lost, a role it has played in my psyche for as long as I can remember.

By this time we were living above my parents' second shop at 138 Bute Street in Treherbert. From here, the curious topographical feature of Penpych loomed large to the north. This is one of Europe's few table-top mountains. I had no kindly uncle or cousin to take me up it and tell me tales of the wondrous happenings that no doubt occurred there back in the mists of Celtic time. It remained for me a mere backdrop to the daily round of school and 'helping out' in the shop. But I do recall thinking how nicely its flat top would accommodate a castle and a handful of romantic ghosts!

The Treherbert shop was set out more or less identically to the one a mile and half down the road in Treorchy, but the living accommodation above it was more spacious. At the back of the shop there was a flight of wooden steps that led down to what we called the 'cellar.' How I hated those steps! My mother had Luigino and me scrub them regularly. The cellar wasn't really a cellar, just a room at a lower level than the shop itself. This was where my father made his ice-cream in large wooden vats. He would rise every morning at five and spend the next few hours preparing the daily ration of fresh ice cream. Beyond this space, another door led outside to the banks of the Rhondda Fawr, which meandered despondently past our back door. But this poor, black and oily body of water was no peer to the sparkling and fresh Ceno that flowed past my mother's home in Barsia di Sotto and was never a playmate for Luigino and I.

My father had rented this shop from fellow Italians by the name of Gazzi, one of the 'pioneering' Bardigiani families who had colonised the valleys along with the Bracchis, the Bernis and the Rabaiottis at the turn of the century. I remember Luigino and I exploring the loft above the shop shortly after we had moved in. Among other things, we discovered a box full of sheet music that the previous owners had left behind. We were highly impressed at such a high level of cultural achievement in fellow Italians and were much in awe of the Gazzis thereafter.

The Gazzis, I imagine, retired to Bardi on the hard-earned proceeds of a generation of work in South Wales. But there was no shortage of other Bardigiani families in Treherbert. In Bute Street alone, the Sidoli family ran two shops. The Rabaiotti Brothers also had a refreshment house in Bute Street and another one in Gwendoline Street. The Canale and Tadecicco families ran confectionery stores just down the road towards Treorchy in Baglan Street. In Treorchy itself, the High Street boasted refreshment rooms run by the Rabaiotti Brothers and the Sidolis, and a confectionery store run by the Rivaris. Then there was the refreshment house run by the Conti family in Station Road. These Italian businesses were known generically as 'Bracchis.' They were named after the pioneering Bracchi family, who had set up what was reportedly the first Italian refreshment house in Aberdare back in the 1890s.

Competition was naturally keen as all these establishments were generally aimed at the same clientele, namely the local miners, and things were tough for them in the 1920s. Back in 1905 when my father had first come to South Wales at the age of fifteen to work for his *padrone* Giacomo Bracchi in Aberdare, the region was booming. He – and a whole generation of fellow Bardigiani – had come in on the back of a rising tide of demand for prime quality Welsh naval steam coal. They found many and faithful customers among the fast-growing work force needed to extract the coal from the valleys. Before the First World War coal from South Wales accounted for an incredible one third of world exports. But by the time my father returned after the Great War, the tide had already turned. Oil was replacing coal across the board. The French market, for example, had been lost as France occupied the coalfields of the Ruhr valley under the terms of the Treaty of Versailles. Welsh coal was becoming dearer to extract than that from other sources. Miners' wages were under pressure and the work force was slowly, but inevitably, contracting. In fact, when I consider it, my mother, father and I arrived in the Rhondda Valley in 1921, which was the very year that its population peaked at around 165,000. From that year onwards it declined steadily and ineluctably. With hindsight, we and our Rhonda Valley refreshment house were on a downhill slope to nowhere from the very outset.

Most of our customers were miners. They had little to spend. Among our regulars I remember Dai Fourpence, so-called because he never spent more than four pence on any particular visit to the shop. There was Sid the Cobbler, who limped and wore a built-up boot and his 'butty' Berwyn, who loved to stand outside the shop on a Sunday morning with his mates betting on the numbers of the trams that came trundling down Bute Street.

Even Thomas Three-farthings, the draper from Bute Street, graced our shop at times. He was so named because all his prices ended with ¾d. Shrewdly, he always claimed he had no farthings in his till and gave change in the form of pins and buttons.

These habitués and their friends would congregate for hours in the shop, chatting away in a mixture of Welsh and English, sipping hot Bovril and smoking Woodbines while they played dominoes or 'tippits.' They played this in teams of three, the teams facing each other across a table. The members of one team passed a penny between them beneath the table top, knocked three times on the underside of the table top when they were ready and then presented their clenched fists, one of which concealed the penny, on top of the table to the other team. Shouts of 'tippit in your left, take your left away' and fists banging on table-tops accompanied the game as the opposing team tried to find the fist concealing the penny.

We had a couple of fruit machines in the shops. These were rented from the Berni Brothers from over the mountain in Merthyr Tydfil. Every now and then two burly Italians in broad-brimmed hats would come to the shop to empty the machine and split the takings with my father. This was one of the few occasions when a hush fell over the shop as the miners watched their hard-earned pennies being shared out among what no doubt to them looked like Chicago mafiosi.

In the mid-twenties around half the people in the Rhondda could still speak Welsh. All could speak English, and they did so with that wonderfully melodious South Wales accent forged from the contacts between the Welsh language itself and the English dialects of the south-east Midlands and the West Country of England as well as the English received pronunciation taught in the valley schools. My mother and father always spoke English with an Italian accent. For some reason, the Welsh accent never rubbed off on them. But Luigino and I spoke like true little Welshmen.

In the first week of August 1928 the National Eisteddfod came to Treorchy, the one and only time it was ever held in the Rhondda valley, which was a great honour and a great event for the town that drew crowds from all around. My mother, who seemed to be becoming the driving force behind the business, insisted that this was a sales opportunity that was not to be missed.

School was out, so it was I that was to do the selling! At the age of not quite eight years, I was decked out with a tray attached to a strap around my neck and sent off to peddle confectionery to the crowds in and around the circle of the Gorsedd Stones. But there was no ice-cream for the Bards. It melted too fast in the summer sun! As far as I can remember, this was the first of the many appearances I was to make as a street vendor later in life.

In 1931 my brother Aldo was born. A happy occasion made even happier for me by the fact that his godparents were to be my parents' friends, Angelo and Maria Carpanini, and that meant a visit from their daughter, the lovely Alma. Although we were still just children, it seemed a foregone conclusion in my young mind that Alma and I would marry one day and live happily ever after in the Rhondda selling fish and chips and ice cream and enjoying endless charabanc outings to Porthcawl whenever we could get time off from managing the spreading empire of Emanuelli-Carpanini chip shops, refreshment houses, temperance bars and confectionery stores.

By the early thirties Luigino and I had passed our school examinations, had left Penyrenglyn Junior School and were attending Pentre Secondary School. This was considered to be one of the better schools in the Valleys and we were both very proud to have gained admission. A fine Victorian building, it stood on the side of the hill overlooking the town and the valley. I remember the school's badge boasted a woodsman's axe on a shield with a red background. The school motto read 'Hog Dy Fwallt' or 'Whet Thy Axe,' an injunction to sharpen our wits.

I think it must have been here that people stopped calling me Ettorino. From now on I was known as Ettore and my brother Luigino was now Louis. Netta James, of course, still called me Etto. Dropping the diminutives was a sure sign that we were growing up.

The teachers at Pentre Sec still populate the stage of my memory. There was Jones the Biologist, who looked like Peter Lorrie, Miss Lewis, who taught geography and was the spitting image of Anna May Wong. There was Miss Vaughan, who taught us French and thought I should be good at it because I was Italian and scolded me bitterly because I wasn't. Above all, there was the terrifying Mr. Pugh, who was all too ready to wield his cane at the slightest hint of insubordination. But he had a saving grace: at the end of the school week he would proclaim 'Boys, I shall read you the next chapter of the world's greatest adventure story – Treasure Island!' With his deep Richard Burton voice he would transport us all briefly out of the valleys and aboard the Hispaniola.

Since the Eisteddfod of 1928 my mother had been constantly on the look-out for more opportunities to generate additional turnover to supplement the meagre intake from the day-to-day business at the cafes. She landed one of her greatest coups by negotiating the 'franchise' to supply confectionery and ices to no less than the prestigious Treherbert Opera House in Station Street. This must have infuriated the Contis, who had a refreshment house in the same street.

The 'Opera House' sounds pretty grand, of course, and rather incongruous for a small mining town of a few thousand souls. And indeed, the Opera House in Station Road Treherbert was more of a variety Hall, staging vaudeville, travelling circuses, showing films and providing a venue for the many Welsh male voice choirs from Treherbert, Treorchy and the rest of South Wales. The audience paid a few pence to get in.

The salesmen for my mother's new business venture were recruited from within the family, in other words Louis and myself. From now on we were to be regular members of the 'sales force.' My mother decked us out with trays that we carried on a strap around our necks, just like the one I'd used for the Eisteddfod, and sent us off to the performances to sell ices and confectionery to the audience during the intervals. For Louis and myself, hawking confectionery wasn't at all a bad way to pass an afternoon. After all, we got to see the shows and films that were shown there for free! But the crowning glory was that we were also allowed backstage to sell to the performers. The behind-the-scenes hustle and bustle I found there inspired an enduring love of the theatre in me. I remember being particularly intrigued by the stage sets. Nor did the actresses' scents and perfumes leave me cold even at that tender age! Sadly, I believe the Opera House burnt down in 1934!

Louis and I were both very happy at Pentre Sec and we felt very much at home in the Rhondda. We were thriving on the diet of pasta, pancakes, ravioli and pastasciutta fed us by our mother. We had more and more friends at school. There was the occasional visit with Netta and her brother to the new Ritz cinema across the road with its fascinating neon lights, the first I had ever seen and which I found simply beautiful. My father would take us there occasionally. He loved Laurel and Hardy, or *Stanlio e Olio* as he called them. I think my mother disapproved. My brother and I had our fairy bikes to get about, ferrying items between the two shops when stocks of this or that ran out.

A very special treat was our father's gift of a ten-volume set of Arthur Mee's *The Children's Encyclopaedia,* which contributed much to our education. I loved the section on 'Colours and Mixing Paints.' Father also took us down to Cardiff to visit the National Museum of Wales. I can still see Pomeroy's Perseus holding out the severed head of Medusa and looking down the flight of steps that dominates the entrance hall. I'd never seen anything like it before.

Unfortunately, the roots we were beginning to put down in Wales were soon to be torn up. Conditions had deteriorated so much in the Rhondda and trade was suffering so badly that not even my mother's business acumen was able to turn the tide. I remember Louis and I hearing furious arguments between our parents. We felt something was afoot. The strikes, the hunger marches, the unemployment, the many departures were taking their toll of the business and no amount of hard work seemed to help. In the late 1920s the kindly James family left the Rhondda and moved to England, where prospects were better. My mother was devastated!

One day in 1932 our parents announced a radical and awesome decision. They were going to emigrate! The five of us were to leave the valleys, and we were to go to a foreign country: England!

I wondered whether I would ever see Alma again.

Myself and Luigino in Treherbert in our Penyrenglyn Junior School uniforms. That's Bob in the middle.

Treherbert Opera House. My first regular sales venue. I loved the back-stage bustle, the scenery and the actresses!

38 A SENSE OF BELONGING

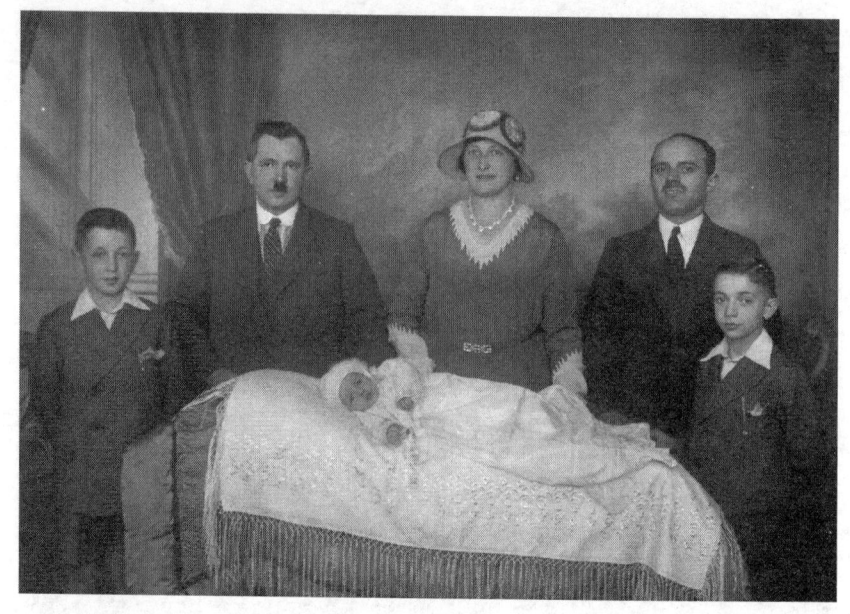

Louis, my father, Maria and Angelo Carpanini and myself in 1931. The baby is my brother Aldo.

School photograph taken towards the end of my career at Penyrenglyn Junior School. I'm the fourth from the right in the second row.

Good-bye Rhondda 39

Regular customers with Louis outside the shop at 81 Bute Street Treorchy in the late 1920s.

A friend, my father, myself and Louis outside the Treorchy shop in the 1920s.

Arthur Delanty and Bob looking after the shop in Treorchy. Time has taken its toll. The lettering is falling off the windows. The fine G. Emanuelli billboard with its gold lettering has gone to be replaced by a temperance bar sign.

CHAPTER 4

A Shakespearean Interlude

*'Ay, now am I in Arden; the more fool I; when I was
at home, I was in a better place: but travellers
must be content.'*
William Shakespeare, As You Like It, Act 4 Scene 2

I do not know by what means, but my parents had become aware of premises in a new building development in that so very English town of Stratford-upon-Avon. The premises consisted of a corner shop and a cafe which was being built on the corner of Birmingham Road and Guild Street. Guild Street, of course, is just around the corner from Shakespeare's birthplace in Henley Street. I imagine this may well have influenced my father's judgement. He would naturally have assumed that the vicinity of the cafe to the 'honey pot' of Shakespeare's birthplace would ensure a steady flow of customers.

And so it was that we found ourselves en route for Stratford-upon-Avon, pinning our hopes on a new beginning in England. Our qualifications from Pentre Sec School allowed both my brother and myself to gain admission to the King Edward VI Grammar School. It was reputedly the school attended by the great Bard himself. This was an 'upper class' boarding and day school and we were supposed to wear stiff collars and a straw boater. Of course, in our straitened circumstances mother could not at that time afford such 'affectations' as she called them and we were, therefore, obliged to attend classes in our everyday clothes, which set us painfully apart from the other boys.

We were not made to feel very welcome at our new school. For one thing we were Italian, spoke with a very pronounced Welsh accent and – to top it all – we were also Catholic. We were not completely alone in our isolation, however. We were joined by two other young brothers. They were Jewish, the sons of a rich local industrialist who owned the firm N.C. Josephs, which ran an aluminium works and a fruit-canning plant. The four of us were made to stand in the corridor outside the classroom when 'Religious Instructions' were being held. The school's headmaster was – needless to say – a 'Reverend.'

The Old School, as it was called, was near the main street and it was in these buildings that Shakespeare is supposed to have learnt his lessons. To the rear were the more modern classrooms and sports facilities. We day-boys were obliged to enter the school from the main street through a gate monitored by a uniformed janitor.

I was sitting one day at one of the very ancient desks in the Old School. The desk was completely covered with initials which had been carved over many years by previous pupils. One set of initials was distinctly W.S. I thought that I would add my own, but before I was able to make any distinct impression on the wooden desk I was discovered by a teacher and very soon brought to book. My punishment was to polish all the benches in the chemistry lab with bees wax.

'The Corner Cafe' – as my father christened his latest venture – was not proving to be much of a success in those early winter months of 1932. There was a scarcity of tourists and we were literally living from hand to mouth.

With the approach of spring, I noticed a marked increase in the number of coaches bringing tourists and especially parties of school children, who were all intent on visiting Shakespeare's birthplace, which was just around the corner from our cafe. This inspired me to write in my best twelve-year-old handwriting dozens of letters to schools in the Rhondda Valley extolling the virtues of father's cafe and inviting them to consider us when thinking of school trips to Stratford. I also emphasised that we were very competitive as regards prices for our teas and so on.

To my joy I received a reply from one of the schools and we made arrangements for the arrival of a busload of hungry and thirsty Welsh school children. The visit was a great success and it was marvellous for my brother and I to hear the children speaking in that melodious Rhondda accent that was still our own.

Our takings were well up that day and father was very pleased. But that, I'm afraid, was my only success, and things did not improve. My mother was increasingly unhappy with Stratford and was missing Wilhelmina and the Rhondda. Although Shakespeare's birthplace was far prettier and more picturesque than the Rhondda, none of us felt we belonged there.

My mother had always kept in touch with the James family ever since they had left the Rhondda in the late 1920s. They had moved to a place called Goldenhill near Tunstall in Stoke-on-Trent, where Tom managed the coop butcher's shop in the Square. Wilhelmina wrote to my mother, singing the praises of 'the Potteries.' She suggested we leave Stratford and join her and Tom in Goldenhill.

My mother needed little persuading and father agreed we should close down the Corner Cafe and move on again. Although Louis and I had never heard of the Potteries, I don't think we were sad to be leaving Stratford.

My first and last English School. King Edward VI Grammar School.

Shakespeare was educated here! Me too! I unwisely carved my initials on one of those desks.

CHAPTER 5

Catering for the Potters

'*The hills and valleys are here by nature beautifully formed, but owe much to the improvement of art. We see here a colony newly-raised in a desert, where clay-built man subsists on clay.*' The Gentleman's Magazine, 1794

I think it must have been in late 1934 or early 1935 that we moved to the Potteries. We stayed with the James family in Goldenhill for several weeks. I shall never forget their kindness during those difficult times. Tom and Wilhelmina were extremely good to us. Poor Netta had to sleep in the bathtub to make room for us. But she didn't take it amiss and was soon taking me to see cowboy movies again, this time at the Ritz cinema, which had just opened down the road in neighbouring Tunstall.

In the meantime, Tom James had located an empty shop at the top of the High Street in Tunstall, which he thought would suit my father's needs. Indeed, my father found the shop very much to his liking even though it had not been occupied for many years and was in a filthy state. It took us some considerable time to clean it up. I believe it had previously accommodated a rag-and-bone business. Next door I remember a Chinese laundry that was run by Mr. Pang, who, I recall, was an inveterate eater of chicken!

My earliest impression of the Potteries, and of Tunstall in particular, was how totally different everything was from

Stratford-upon-Avon. There were no tourists, no souvenir shops, no chocolate-box thatched cottages, no picturesque river meandering between banks shaded by weeping willows. I remember blackened skies, dense smoke belching from the bottle chimneys of the many pottery kilns, cloth-capped potters with clay-splattered aprons, pottery girls with their cheerful banter, a strange dialect. The streets were busy with workers from the neighbouring pot banks of H & R Johnson Tiles, Johnson Bros' Alexandra Works, Enoch Wedgwood and W.H. Grindley. And there were the familiar cloth-capped colliers again, waiting in the High Street for buses to take them to the pits that surrounded the town! Although Tunstall made a grimy impression, in many ways it was so similar to the Rhondda that soon we all felt far more at home than we ever had in the 'refined' Stratford-upon-Avon. What's more, beneath its grime the town was throbbing with activity and creativity, and that was good for business.

In preparation for our new venture I had produced a poster advertising the imminent opening of 'John's Temperance Bar,' offering teas, refreshments, cakes and confectionery. John, obviously, was my father, who had adopted the name given him by the Welsh miners back in the Rhondda for his new shop in Tunstall.

Trade was slow to start, but then – driven perhaps by curiosity – the girls from the pottery factory in Keele Street started to come in for the cakes and Cornish pasties that my mother had started to bake. Men from the slaughter house, also in Keele Street, came in for their morning coffee-break. Gradually we found that trade was increasing and that we had been accepted. Father had started making his ice cream again, and workers on their way home from work would call in for a wafer.

My father had hinted that he was still paying off the rates arrears that he had incurred during our time in the Rhondda Valley, both at Treorchy and Treherbert, so we remained financially stretched. But this did not stop my father enjoying the occasional visit to the Ritz cinema. The Ritz seated an audience of 1,600 and my father was often among them. His favourites were still Laurel and Hardy, who could send him into thigh-slapping fits of laughter. My mother disapproved strongly of his frivolous 'cinéphile' habits and when he had been gone from the shop for too long she would send my brother Aldo off to find him. In those days, smoking was still permitted in the cinema and as an inveterate smoker my father took full advantage of this. The wreaths of blue cigar smoke coiling above him in the beam of the light cast by the projector would immediately betray his whereabouts in the darkened cinema and made it easy for Aldo to locate him among the audience.

My school career had sadly ended in Stratford and – in order to supplement the family income – I took a job at the Gordon Pottery works of A.G. Richardson and Co. in Pinnox Street, Tunstall. I must have been 14 years of age at the time. I was employed as a so-called lodge-boy. This involved weighing the lorries as they brought in supplies of coal for the pottery kilns. I also made myself generally useful by carrying messages between various works managers. This allowed me to see many different departments of the works. I loved going into the decorating shops even though the pottery girls teased me mercilessly because of my strange Welsh accent. I loved the smell of the gilders' gold and the banders' painting materials, and I admired the cheerful designs of the jugs and bowls. Only recently did I realise that these were the work of the celebrated pottery designer, Charlotte Rhead. Just down the road, Clarice Cliff was also producing her now-famous art deco and Bizarre ware at the Newport Pottery in neighbouring Burslem. The Potteries really were a very creative place, despite the grime.

I was only paid 7 shillings and nine pence a week as a lodge-boy so I was glad to hear of a job paying a handsome 10 shillings a week working for Thomas and Evans, a company which – coincidentally – was headquartered back in the Rhondda. They produced the famous Corona brand of soft drinks at their Welsh Hills works in Porth. They also had a fleet of vans in Longport in the Potteries and it was my job to go out on one of them with a driver. We knocked on the doors of houses in the new Little Chell estate, delivering wooden crates of beverages and corona 'pop.' We also tried to book orders from new customers. I remember a new van being delivered from the company's headquarters in Porth. The Welsh driver who had brought it up from the Rhondda was inordinately proud of the vehicle, which was brand new, bright red and adorned with beautiful gold lettering. I have always been interested in design, calligraphy and 'lettering' and so it was with perhaps more-than-average attention that I examined the company's livery on the side of the van. It read *Thomas Ltd and Evans*. That can't be right, I thought. I drew the driver's attention to the error. 'Shouldn't that read *Thomas and Evans Ltd*?' I asked. 'Damn! You're right! I'll have to take her all the bloody way back to Porth!' he replied.

It was not long, however, before the family catering and ice-cream business really began to take off and it was time for me to leave the job in the pot bank to help out. Both Louis and myself were recruited to hawk our father's ice cream around the streets of Tunstall and Goldenhill, pushing handcarts. My brother and I detested this, but we could not complain because even our mother stood outside Tunstall Park Gates with a handcart she had improvised from an old pram. She was often told to move on by the local police, but this did not deter her from trying to make an honest living for the family.

Yes, I hated and resented those days, pushing my ice-cream cart in all weathers around the streets of Tunstall. I resented it and envied youths of my age who were free to enjoy themselves and were benefiting from an education while my brother and I were compelled to ply the humiliating trade of street vendor. I was torn between loyalty to the family and my own inclinations. If I had been free to follow the latter, I should have been happy to stay in the pottery industry. Perhaps I might have been able to put my love of painting and design to better use there.

I was, however, becoming ever more deeply involved in the family business, replying to suppliers and corresponding with the local authorities with regard to health regulations and so on. My mother had never been to school although the force of circumstance had turned her into an astute business woman and with Wilhelmina's help she had learnt to read and write English. Nevertheless, she preferred to leave the business correspondence to me and Louis.

In 1937 England celebrated the coronation of King George VI. This was a great boost to business, with crowds and parades filing past our shop in the High Street. My father had decided to contribute to the street decorations by hanging an Italian flag from the first-floor windows. With my mother's help I managed to make him one. In those days, the Italian flag still sported the arms of the House of Savoy, and seemed suitably royal for the occasion and a fine tribute from one royal house to the other. Next door, Mr. Pang said he'd like to do the same, but he didn't have a Chinese flag. They were even harder to come by than Italian flags. So I produced a Chinese flag, too, which – if I remember rightly – was red and blue with a white star in the corner. It matched rather nicely the countless Union Flags that were on display.

My mother, who loved everything royal, was very enthusiastic about the coronation celebrations. 'Boys, we gotta do something special,' she said. 'What do you suggest Ma?' asked Louis. 'Well on the day, you gonna distribute ice creams to the crowds in the street – FOR FREE!' Louis and I looked at her in disbelief. My mother never missed the opportunity to make an extra penny. She'd break up bars of chocolate into bits and sell it in the cafe at a hefty premium as 'Broken Chocolate.' 'FREE Ma? Are you sure?' 'Sì, sì, sì! I'm sure. Is'a good marketing trick!' She smiled shrewdly. I think that must have been one of the last times Louis and I appeared on the streets of Tunstall with an ice-cream cart. And it was no doubt one of our most popular appearances!

Later the same year at the age of seventeen I took and passed my driving test, and things began to take a turn for the better. With my driving licence in my pocket, my father purchased the firm's first motorised ice-cream van. Even after more than seventy years I can still remember its registration number: FVT 348! The acquisition of this van finally put an end to the street-hawking career which I had started as a schoolboy selling ice cream from a tray to the patrons of the Opera House in Treherbert and of the Eisteddfod in Treorchy and which I had resumed as a reluctant teenager with an ice-cream cart in the streets of Tunstall. I felt that I was climbing out of the bottom division and entering the second division, and hoped I might be heading for better things.

Leaving the familiar streets of Tunstall behind me in FVT 348, I was now able to reach new customers further afield. I delighted in establishing my round among the villages of the North Staffs and Cheshire areas: Congleton, Mow Cop, Newchapel, Packmoor, Harriseahead, Scholar Green/Ackers Crossing, and many others. I would announce my arrival in what seemed to me in those days remote areas by blowing my two-tone horn, which replaced the usual motor horn. Hearing my approach, customers would be waiting for me at my recognised stopping place. I did good business. The two-tone horn was later replaced by the now musical chimes that were to become a familiar feature of ice-cream vans. My beloved FVT 348 was built by Ford and had been very expertly converted to our specifications by the Tunstall-based firm of coach builders and painters, Stoker Brothers of Sneyd Street.

Within a very short time we purchased a second van, which was operated by my brother Louis. He also established his own round in the Butt Lane and Kidsgrove areas, where he was very well accepted and popular. As we gradually added to our fleet of vans we adopted our corporate colour-scheme of orange, cream and chocolate, my mother's favourite colours. The finishing touch was a representation of Bardi Castle, expertly painted by Stoker Brothers, who took great pride in their work. The Bardi-Castle motif was to remain the logo for our business for many years to come, adorning not only our vehicles, but also our company letterheads.

Catering for the Potters

As a family, we all worked very hard and took a great deal of pride in our products and how we presented ourselves. My father, Louis and I wore white jackets with orange collars and cuffs, with the name 'EMANUELS' emblazoned on our breast pockets. In the meantime, my father had bought his first car. This was a Hillman Minx saloon, dove-grey in colour. They say that one always remembers one's first car. I always remember my first ice-cream van, the FVT 348! But I also remember father's first car with affection. Its registration number was the unforgettable GGO 216!

A car means freedom, of course, and in 1938 my father decided we should use it to take a trip back down to South Wales to visit his old friend Angelo Carpanini. My mother generously offered to look after the shop for a couple of days so Louis and I could go with him. I was delighted as this would give me a chance to see Alma again, whom I'd never forgotten in the five years or so since we had left Wales. I was also pleased because my father let me drive.

So we 'motored down' to Aberdare from Tunstall in the dove-grey Hillman Minx while my mother looked after the shop. Angelo was out on business when we arrived, but his wife Maria was at home. She was busily engaged in opening a shoal of letters. She explained that as a sideline – she said it was her 'pin money' – she kept a fleet of caravans in Porthcawl. She rented these out during the summer months. The letters were applications for caravan bookings. Every so often she would tear one up and throw it into the bin. 'Why did you do that?' I asked. 'Well, if they can't bother to enclose a stamped addressed envelope' she said with a laugh, 'they have no chance of renting one of my caravans!'

Alma was there, too, and so was her sister Irene. They had, of course, both grown up a lot since I had last seen them, and were now attractive young ladies! Alma had become an accomplished piano-accordionist. She got out her instrument and played us all a tune. I think it was some romantic Italian stuff. Romantic is difficult to do on an accordion, but it struck love into my heart all the same! I was infatuated from that moment on. And I thought I caught a glimpse of reciprocity in Alma's eye's. 'Maybe it's my new suit and the dove-grey car!' I thought. Angelo was inordinately proud of his daughter, and told my father what a very able pastry cook she was, specialising in apple tarts, which were very popular in her father's restaurant. I saw before me the perfect wife-to-be!

Maria Carpanini enjoyed our visit so much she didn't want it to end. So much so in fact that she virtually invited herself for a stay in the Potteries. 'Come on Etto my love,' she said (like Alma and Netta, she called me Etto) 'take me up to see your mother, I'm dying for a chat with her.' So I drove what I earnestly thought would be my future mother-in-law up to see my mother in Tunstall.

She sang all the way from Aberdare to Tunstall, her favourite song being Ramona, which she repeated over and over again. She truly was a fun-loving person. Every year she would take her annual holiday in Blackpool. She always went alone. I'm sure she had a good time while Angelo and his daughters kept the business running!

Later that year my father took off for Italy with my brother Louis. They had both fallen in love with Victoria Arduino! Although very curvaceous, this was not a lady, but a huge and elaborate coffee-making machine that my father felt was a must for the business. I think he might have been egged on in this by his friend Tom James, who loved all things technical. I had seen them pouring over glossy magazines with pictures of the machine and heard them discussing the specifications of the various versions. The trip took Louis and my father to Milan, where they ordered the machine for delivery later that year. They then took the opportunity to go to Bardi to visit friends and family. They sent us postcards of the castle and the town, which re-awakened my nostalgia for the place and revived my desire to go back to that enchanted spot.

Hardly had my father and Louis returned to Tunstall than the Victoria Arduino turned up in a huge crate. It was a splendid sight. Almost a meter high and weighing 70 kilos it glistened and shone, a masterpiece in chrome. Though topped by a silver spread-eagle, with its sensuous curves it was more of a Venus than a Victoria! Unfortunately, with its pipes and pressure gauges, its hot-water and steam wands it was just too much for the local plumbers. If taken into operation, they said, they couldn't guarantee it wouldn't explode. So the beautiful Victoria Arduino never served a cup of coffee in our shop. Nevertheless, she was always a great eye-catcher and a major embellishment.

By all counts, by the late 1930s, business was booming and things were really looking up. My father had stepped up his ice-cream production to meet the growing demand. For the same reason, we had expanded the business premises in the High Street, adding a two-floor corner-shop that used to be a bicycle store and was adjacent to the original premises at number 125 High Street. We called the whole thing the 'Wonder Bar.' So 'John's Temperance Bar and Refreshment House,' which by then was beginning to sound a little old fashioned, ceased to exist.

We decorated the new Wonder Bar lovingly. I remember painstakingly painting a frieze of foliage and grapes around the top of the walls in the upstairs rooms. As I painted in the silence of the new shop, I fondly recalled Zio Pain' chatting to me as he decorated the baptistery in Cereseto more than a decade earlier. The childhood dreams of becoming a painter that he had awakened in me back in Bardi were still with me as a teenager in Tunstall. How I still yearned to pursue a different career, to become a designer, a graphic artist, a painter, a set-designer in the theatre, anything but an ice-cream vendor! How happy I was painting the rooms in the new cafe, designing stationery, logos and posters for the business and how miserable I was when I had to sell ice cream on the streets of Tunstall. But for some reason, I never dared put all this before my parents. It was a tacit assumption that Louis and I should work for the family business and one that neither of us dared challenge. The firm of 'Emanuel &

Sons' was our protective nest, but also a prison for our true ambitions.

In due course the work on the Wonder Bar was finished and it was not long before the new premises were also full of customers. Young people loved it. They didn't go to pubs in those days and binge-drinking was unheard of.

I began to see a brighter future for our family business where hawking ice cream on the streets would be a thing of the past and where hard work would offer a real prospect of building up a chain of cafes and a vast fleet of modern ice-cream vans that would bring affluence and a true sense of belonging for the whole family. I was beginning to feel very much at home in the Potteries.

Catering for the Potters 55

Our new hometown was not exactly pretty, but it was a good place to do business.

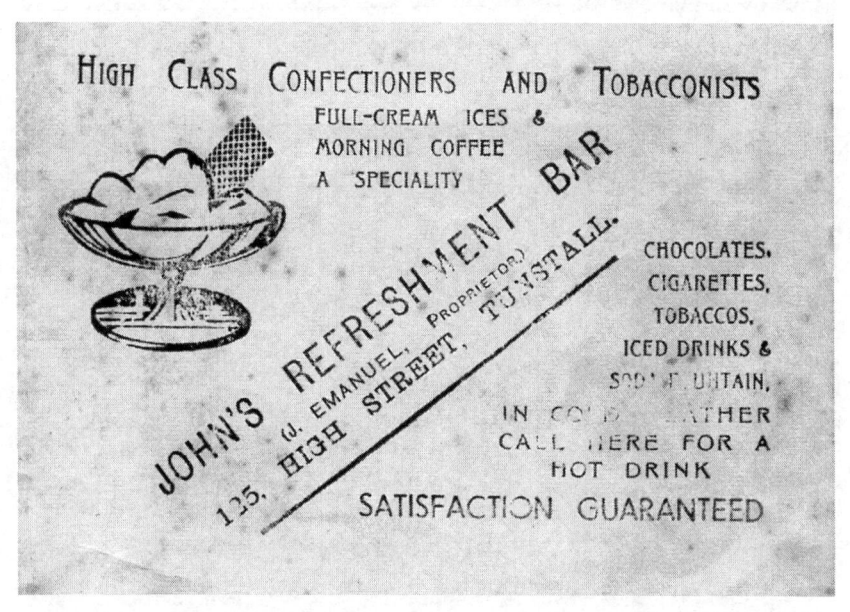

Early advertising for 'John's Refreshment Bar.' We changed the name later to 'The Wonder Bar.'

56 A SENSE OF BELONGING

My father in the doorway of our first cafe at 125 High Street Tunstall. The little boy is my brother Aldo.

Business is booming. Louis, myself, my father and Aldo with our first ice-cream van, the much-loved FVT 348. This picture was taken in the late 1930s. My father's ice cream had just won the Diploma of Merit at Olympia in 1937.

*From 1938 onwards, a beautiful Victoria Arduino 'macchina per caffè' graced the Wonder Bar.
(Photograph courtesy of Nuova Simonelli spa).*

Three brothers: Louis, Aldo and myself in the mid-1930s.

CHAPTER 6

Mussolini: His Part in My Downfall

'The regime had created an imaginary Spartan country, in which all men had to make believe they were heroic soldiers, all women Roman matrons, all children Balilla (the Genoa street urchin who started a revolt against the Austrian garrison in 1746 by throwing one stone). This was done by means of slogans, flags, stirring speeches from balconies, military music, mass meetings, parades, dashing uniforms, medals, hoaxes, and constant distortions of reality.' Luigi Barzini, The Europeans

Clouds had been gathering on the Anglo-Italian political horizon all through the 1930s and sentiment had been souring towards Italians in Britain at least since 1935 when Mussolini invaded Abyssinia and the League of Nations imposed sanctions on Italy. Thankfully, however, our family was left unscathed by the growing unpopularity of fascists and Italians. Our customers remained faithful to us and business continued as normal.

As a teenager I was thoroughly apolitical. I was hardly aware of Mussolini's territorial ambitions in France and Africa and almost completely ignorant of his domestic policies. True, I had heard our parish priest, Father Ryan, denounce Mussolini's invasion of Albania in May 1939, but this had not made any lasting impression on me. I probably had little idea where Albania was. But I knew Mussolini was a dictator. Whenever my mother got too bossy, which she did from time to time, my father would shrug his shoulders, cast his eyes to the ceiling and proclaim 'Carolina ha sempre ragione!' ('Carolina is always right.' This was modelled on the fascist slogan 'Mussolini ha sempre ragione!')

Though indifferent to contemporary Italian politics, I had become increasingly sensitive to my Italian cultural heritage and was eager to know more of Italy's art, history, literature and especially its language. I had begun to read Dante, Manzoni and Ariosto, but only in English translation, of course. This I found frustrating and was, therefore, eager to learn the language so that I could read Italian authors in the original. When at home, my parents still talked together in the Bardigiano dialect and this was the only sort of Italian of which I had any command at all. I noticed, however, that whenever we had visits from fellow Italians they would put on their 'telephone' voice and lapse into 'il vero italiano' or 'the true Italian.' As the Italians say *'lingua toscana in bocca romana.'* In other words, 'the Tuscan tongue as spoken by the Romans.' I suppose you might call this the equivalent of our Queen's English.

This was the kind of Italian I wished to learn and so I enrolled in an Italian postal tuition course with *Radio Italiana*. All very well, of course, but correspondence courses are not much help with diction and correct pronunciation. I began to think a trip to Italy would be the solution – if only I could afford it.

Since the mid-1920s, many large British cities had had a so-called *Fascio* or *Casa d'Italia*. These were initially social clubs for Italians that had evolved from earlier organisations such as the Dante Alighieri Society. On the surface, their remit was to foster Italian culture and language among the Italian community in the UK. Their activities included recruiting the children of Italian immigrants for trips to Italy. The secretary of the *Fascio* of Manchester, a Signor Floriani, called at our cafe in Tunstall. Hearing of my interest in Italy and things Italian, he informed us that the Italian government was organising a *'campo estivo'* – a summer camp – at Rome and Pescara. Naturally, the offer was sponsored by the Italian authorities. Financially, its terms were exceptionally seductive, with 'no strings attached,' seductive enough for my parents to agree to my going.

So it was that in the summer of 1939 the opportunity arose for me to visit Italy for a month-long holiday in order – or so I thought – to improve my command of the Italian language and my knowledge of Italian culture and history. Blithely naive about what was hidden behind the word 'Fascio,' I enthusiastically enrolled on what I thought would be the chance of a lifetime. How wrong I was, and how I was to regret this decision later!

This was supposed to be a month-long holiday, all expenses paid, with opportunities to visit museums and art galleries, and simply to enjoy the Italian way of life. This – I thought – was what I had always been looking for – a chance not to be missed.

It was August 1939 and I was eighteen years of age. I travelled by train across France as part of a small contingent of British 'Italians.' Had I known that the French would be at war with the Germans just a month later, I would undoubtedly have stayed at home. As it was, after a two-day trip I arrived safely at Monte Sacro, a rather dreary Roman suburb.

On arrival, our British contingent was merged with similar groups of young Hungarians, French, Greeks and Poles. Most did not speak Italian, or very little.

The very name of the camp – 'Campo Mussolini' – augured ill. Large billboards proclaimed slogans coined by the Duce: *'In Africa c'è posto e gloria per tutti* – In Africa there's room and glory for all!,' *'Guerra – una parola che non ci fa paura* – War – a word that does not frighten us,' *'Abbiamo dei conti vecchi e nuovi da regolare* – we have some old and new accounts to settle' and of course *'Credere, Obbedire, Combattere* – Believe, Obey, Fight!'

To my horror, we were promptly herded into tents and it began to dawn on me that this was not a holiday venue, but a pseudo-military training camp run according to fascist principles. We were issued with the uniforms of the so-called *'avanguardisti.'* The *avanguardisti* were part of the paramilitary youth organisation cooked up by the fascists on the lines of Baden-Powell's scouts back in the twenties. Miserable in my scratchy and bedraggled uniform, I felt that I had been completely duped by Signor Floriani.

Days were long and arduous and we were made to march up and down, slope and present arms with antiquated rifles – without ammunition of course. All the usual military business. We 'marched' through the local streets to a military band, but there was nothing military about us. We must have looked a rather pathetic sight, a juvenile version of Dad's Army, perhaps.

During our stay in Monte Sacro, we saw nothing of the city of Rome although it was only a short bus-ride away. Then, after a couple of weeks of playing soldiers in Campo Mussolini we were informed we were to spend a week at the seaside resort of Pescara on the other side of the peninsula. My spirits rose briefly. 'The seaside can't be worse than this,' I thought.

After a long and hot ride across the peninsula in a train fitted with hard wooden seats, we arrived at the camp at Pescara. This was located in the Pineta d'Annunzio – a wooded area named after the Pescara-born poet and novelist much loved by the fascists for his bombastic nationalism, among other things. Pescara turned out to be a sea-side version of Monte Sacro. Like Monte Sacro we were accommodated in another *'tendopoli,'* a city of tents, but this time the tents were lined up below pine trees. We were issued with a new uniform. Because we were at the seaside we were given a naval-style outfit this time, very much like an English Sea Scouts uniform. Pescara turned out to be no better than Monte Sacro. There was more of the same pointless marching and parading.

On our return to Rome we were told that we were to receive a visit by a group of Hitler Youth and that we were to make them welcome. They duly arrived resplendent in their immaculate brown uniforms with their white, red and black swastika armbands. They were all blond, tanned, muscular, all the same height and a formidable sight! At morning roll-call they assembled outside their tents with all their equipment and kit laid out in perfect symmetry. Needless to say, we 'Italians' did not fraternise with them, especially when we were told that the object of all our drilling was to take part in a 'group performance' before Benito Mussolini.

But this did not come to pass as on the 3 September, France and Great Britain declared war on Germany, and Mussolini no doubt had more important things to do. There was not even enough time to issue us with a new uniform and we spent the last days in the camp in the sailor uniforms we had been issued at Pescara. The tents were dismantled, the camp disbanded.

The frontiers were closed and we were in the hands of the Italian government. Rumours were rife that we might be held for enlistment in the Italian army. These were scary days. The authorities announced that all those campers who had relatives living in Italy would be allowed to make their way to them until such time as the necessary arrangements could be made for them to return to the UK on a group passport.

The only pleasant memory that I have of my experience of the camp at Monte Sacro was the early-morning ablutions that took place in the open air along a row of steel washbasins where the icy cold spring-water tasted just like champagne. Otherwise, the weeks I spent there and at Pescara were some of the most distressing, frustrating and unhappy of my life and looking back I realise what a foolish and ill-informed decision I had made in accepting the offer of what I assumed would have been an educational and rewarding experience, but which had turned out to be a complete hoax.

I decided to make my way to my grandfather's farm in Bardi. The camp commandant issued me with a travel warrant with the stipulation that I travel in uniform to my destination. Another instance of fascist bombast, I thought.

With my limited knowledge of Italian geography, I worked out that if I took the train from Rome to Piacenza I might with luck be able to get to Bardi by bus as I knew that there was no railway station at Bardi. This I did, but on eventually reaching Piacenza I found that there was a wait of some six hours for a bus to Bardi. I took this as an opportunity to change out of my silly sailor suit and into civilian clothes. I felt it would be most incongruous, anyway, to arrive in the Apennines wearing a Sea Scout's uniform. I stuffed it into the bottom of my bag, where it was to stay until I eventually got home. I was breaking the first fascist rule 'Obey' and who knows what trouble I might have been in had anyone checked my papers. I do not remember much about Piacenza. I do know, however, that a Botticelli Madonna that used to hang in the Castello di Bardi is now in the museum there. For safekeeping so to speak! Or that, at least, is what the Piacentini say.

It was almost dark when I finally arrived in Bardi. It hadn't changed much since 1927, except for the brand-new Neo-Romanesque church, which now – having been built in the fascist era – symbolically faced Piazza della Vittoria and turned its flank haughtily to the Piazza del Mercato and the church of Giovanni Battista. The problem now was to reach my grandfather's farm. The family had moved since my first visit and was no longer living at Barsia di Sotto. They had taken a farm at Cogno di Grezzo, which lay a little way out of town, but still within sight of the castle. Seeing my predicament, a kind Bardigiano took me on his ox cart to my grandfather Giovanni's farm.

Nonno Giovanni was smoking the last mezzo toscano of the day when I arrived. I was greeted with open arms. Zio Toni made jokes about how I had grown since my first visit some twelve years before. There followed a very welcome and hearty meal, washed down with a bottle of barbera as I told my family the story of my stay at Campo Mussolini. They grumbled about the 'Duce' and his policies. He had turned the country into a battlefield! He had fought a 'Battle for Grain,' a 'Battle for Land,' a 'Battle for the Lira' and even a 'Battle for Babies', everything was a battle! But he hadn't won any yet. And now he was planning a war! And the taxes! He'd even put an extra tax on bachelors so they'd get married and have children. He wanted more children so he'd have more soldiers to play with when he took on France and England, they moaned.

Despite the warmth of my reception in Bardi and the hospitality I received, I was naturally dejected after my camp experiences, and during the two months or so that I was to spend at Grezzo I was greatly concerned. My parents at home were worried about me, and I was troubled that I might never get back to England.

Frequent letters and telegrams were the order of the day. Twice a week I visited the municipio in Bardi to check if there was any news about my repatriation to the UK. My mind was unsettled and I was unable to enjoy to the full my stay with Nonno Giovanni. Zio Toni and my cousins did all they could for me, for which I was extremely grateful. To fill the hours I would help out on the farm, accompanying my uncle Toni when he ploughed the fields with his oxen. He showed me how to spray the vines with sulphur to stop mildew on the grapes, he taught me the names of all the grape varieties. Sad to say, today I can only distinguish white from black. I do remember, however, that one of the varieties, a little black grape called *tintura,* was used to bring a rich ruby colour to the finished wine. At night we would gather outside on the patio where my cousins and I would strip the leaves from the maize which had been harvested. The maize was then sent for milling.

Before I left Bardi I witnessed another show of fascist pomp. In those days, the Italians celebrated the end of the First World War on 4 November. This was the date that the peace treaty was signed with the defeated Austro-Hungarian Empire in 1918. On this day in 1939 the flags were out in Bardi. I looked on as black-shirts dressed up like Mussolini and uniformed ballila children marched through the town with

Musardi the mayor and the town band. The procession ended at Piazza della Vittoria, where in front of the war memorial commemorating the Italian soldiers who had fallen between 1915 and 1918, they gave the fascist salute to Mussolini and the king, Vittorio Emanuele III. The mood was sober.

When news finally came from the municipio in Bardi that permission had been given for me to return home I was both elated and yet sad to be leaving good friends and my mother's family after all that they had done for me. So it was with tears and sadness mixed with relief to be going home that I left Cogno di Grezzo and Bardi, this only for the second time in my life, a visit I shall always recall with happiness mixed with anxiety.

Little did I know it then, but almost a decade and a world war were to pass before I was to be able to visit Bardi again.

Winged Victory strides resolutely forward between rows of tents holding aloft the letter 'M' for Mussolini!

The 'summer camp' in Pescara intended for young 'avanguardisti' recruited from families of Italians abroad.

A telegram I sent from Bardi in November 1939 reassuring my parents that all was fine.

Postcard from C. Floriani, Secretary of the Fascio of Manchester, informing my parents of my arrival at Victoria Station on 22 November 1939.

CHAPTER 7

'Collar the Lot!'

'The power of the Executive to cast a man into prison without formulating any charge known to the law, and particularly to deny him the judgement of his peers, is in the highest degree odious and is the foundation of all totalitarian government whether Nazi or Communist.' Winston Churchill

The journey back to the UK through France was tense. The 'drôle de guerre' – the phoney war – was already nearly three months old. French and British troops were waiting for the Germans to attack. During the Channel crossing we felt we were running the gauntlet of German submarines. Finally, I disembarked from the train at Victoria Station and headed for Euston, and on to Stoke-on-Trent.

The dove-grey Hillman Minx was waiting outside the station, inside it my mother and father. I was overjoyed to see them! At last I was home!

Britain had, however, changed a good deal since I had left in August. I remember sandbags, barrage balloons, tin hats, gasmasks, military uniforms and a growing fear of invasion by the Germans. The first reports of German planes being downed by Spitfires were coming in, which inspired pride in Potteries people: the designer of the Spitfire, Reginald Mitchell, came from Kidsgrove, which is near Goldenhill.

It was good to be able to immerse myself in the family business in Tunstall again and to forget all the marching, parading and fears I'd experienced in Italy. The daily routine of was very welcome. Our family business struggled as milk and sugar rationing were introduced in early 1940 and ingredients for our ice-cream production became scarce. My brother Louis was drafted into the army and by April he was fighting in the Norwegian campaign. Aldo was still at school. I was expecting to be drafted any time. Alma came up to visit us in Tunstall. I remember picking her up in the Hillman-Minx at Kidsgrove Station and taking her to the pictures at the Regent Cinema in Hanley, where we had tea together in the tea-rooms after the film. She was fashionably dressed and looked very striking with her dark ringlets and Italian looks. I was very proud to be seen together with her. She still called me Etto and I still had a 'crush' on her.

Italy remained neutral although the Italians living in the UK were becoming increasingly anxious that Mussolini would drag it into war on Hitler's side, but they continued to hope against the odds that he would at least remain on the sidelines.

The catastrophe came on 10 June 1940 when Italy finally declared war on the Allies. This was a tragic day for all Italians living and working in the United Kingdom, and in Italy, too, come to that. At a stroke, virtually all adult male Italians living in the UK were arrested and interned. Churchill had allegedly issued the order to 'collar the lot!' Many of the Italians who were arrested were shopkeepers, cafe proprietors, chefs, waiters, artists, musicians, priests and ironically those who had fled the fascist regime to seek refuge in Britain. My father, who was still an Italian citizen in 1940, was spared because he had been resident in the United Kingdom for more than twenty years.

In some areas, local citizens became hostile. Shop windows were smashed and the contents looted. Thankfully, however, my parents did not suffer. The authorities did, however, inflict some restrictions on the family. My father was still an Italian national and had only been spared internment because he had been resident in the United

Kingdom for more than twenty years. As far as the authorities were concerned, however, he was still a potential fifth-columnist and he was singled out for special treatment: his car was immobilised – the rotor-arm was removed from the engine and the vehicle was mothballed for the duration of the war – and his radio was confiscated. Apart from these minor inconveniences, life continued more or less as normal and my parents were able to keep the business going.

But my stay at the summer camp at Monte Sacro in Rome had not gone unnoticed by the authorities, and they had taken it very seriously. On the evening of the 10 June 1940 I was visited by two plain-clothed officers from Hanley Police Station. They showed me an order for my arrest, informing me that I was to be detained under section 18B of the Defence of the Realm Act. I was deemed to be a British subject 'of hostile associations' and a potential threat to national security! My parents were aghast. The officers instructed me to get some clothes. They followed me upstairs to my room. While I collected some things together they searched my room. They found my sailor's uniform from Pescara. This sealed my fate. Later, at my indictment on October 24 that year, I was accused of being in possession of a fascist uniform!

I was taken to Hanley Police Station. This turned out to be the first of many places of detention I was to be held in. The next day I was moved to Walton Prison in Liverpool, where I was to spend the next seven weeks. We were housed in D Wing, a part of the prison which had not been used since the days of the Suffragettes. It was in a filthy condition. Pigeon excrement seemed to be everywhere.

I was there during the 'Christmas Blitz' of 1940, when hundreds died during several days of bombing just before Christmas. I was in cell number 16 on the fifth-floor landing. Being bombed is always scary, but it's really terrifying when you're locked up! Porridge was served to us in battered aluminium basins. To this day I have a dislike of it. The bedtime cocoa that was served with a slice of bread formed a layer of cocoa butter if left to cool. We made candles which we used after 'lights out.' Slopping out in the mornings was a very degrading experience and something I will always remember.

In July 1940, while still detained at Liverpool, I heard the terrible news of the sinking of the Arandora Star. On July 1 1940, the steamship had left Liverpool bound for Canada. On board were 1,562 internees, 764 of these were Italians, many of whom were Bardigiani from South Wales. There were also German and Italian Jewish refugees and some German prisoners of war on board. The Italians were housed below decks and the Germans on the top deck, which was surrounded by barbed wire. The ship was headed for Canada, where the passengers were to be held in internment camps.

On 2 July 1940 at 7:00 a.m. the ship was torpedoed by the German U-Boat U47 commanded by Captain Günther Prien, known as the 'Bull of Scapa Flow.' He had also sunk HMS Royal Oak in October 1939. The Arandora Star was 125 miles west of the Irish coast and sank within 30 minutes. Over 800 lives were lost, including many Italians and 46 Bardigiani from South Wales. This terrible event is still commemorated every year at the Arandora Star Memorial Chapel in Bardi cemetery.

On 31 July we left Walton Prison, destination unknown. I remember we were being booed and jeered in the streets as we made our way to the railway station. After the sinking of the Arandora Star, we were all hoping and praying that we were not heading for a transport ship. We travelled by train and under military escort.

Our destination turned out to be Ascot, where we were 'accommodated' in the winter quarters of the Bertram Mill's Circus, situated on the outskirts of the town and surrounded by pine trees. We were put up in various buildings, including the elephant houses.

Administration appeared to be non-existent and no provision was made to feed us. We had not eaten since leaving Liverpool. It was very hot and we were made to strip naked and line up in rows for a roll call. Several of the older internees fainted. Many of the Italians had catering skills, they took over the kitchens, scrubbed some old boilers and soon had a passable vegetable soup. I imagine there must have been between four and five hundred men at the Ascot camp, a mixture of British fascists, Germans, Italians, Jews, Hungarians, Irish, Welsh, Scots and English. There were even some communists. Over the next few weeks conditions improved and we settled down, although we did not know what the future held in store for us. During my ten weeks at Ascot I made a few friends. One was Carlo Rossi, proprietor of the Beacon Hotel in Bristol. He was an avid reader of historical novels and was never happier than with a Raphael Sabatini paperback. Two other friends were the Rietti brothers, young Jewish Italians. Bobby Rietti is now Sir Robert Rietti! They were formidable actors and kept us entertained on many occasions.

In mid-November we were told we were to move again. Rumours were rife that we were to be shipped to Canada or Australia, with all the attendant dangers. We left Ascot on 18 November. Thankfully, we were not heading for a transport ship, but for the racecourse at York! An internment camp had been improvised there in the main grandstand and administration buildings. Everything was again surrounded by barbed wire and patrolled by military guards. We were accommodated beneath and at the back of the grandstand. In some cases these were very cramped quarters. My main recollection of York is the boiled rice, which seemed to dominate the main meals. It was sometimes enlivened by the aroma of chocolate from the nearby Terry's chocolate factory. We spent some sixteen weeks in York, and left on 14 March 1941. Our destination was again kept from us.

This time it turned out to be Huyton, a suburb of Liverpool. The camp there consisted of a half-completed council housing estate. There were some four rows of semi-derelict council houses. Rubble was scattered all over the place. We were issued with battered aluminium dinner plates which had seen better days. We used builders' sand to scour them. I can remember supplementing our greens with the dandelion leaves which grew in abundance on the four acres or so of land that surrounded the houses. The camp was enclosed by barbed wire again, but this time there were also anti-aircraft guns, which sometimes made it very difficult to sleep at night. Working parties were occasionally sent out of the camp to help clear up bomb damage. One of my fellow detainees, whom I recall with pleasure, is Mario Collaccico, a Stephen Fry look-alike, who had a fine sense of humour and wit and who kept our spirits up during our stay at Huyton. We left Huyton Camp on 12 May 1941.

The word on the grapevine was that we were to be sent to the Isle of Man. I looked forward to this with some relief as I felt that perhaps my wanderings would then be over. We were taken under strict escort to Liverpool, where we boarded the 'Lady of Mann.' As the ship set sail for Douglas, the detainees quickly renamed it 'H.M. Prison Ship the Lady of Mann' due to the large number of military guards and the fact that we were to be escorted throughout the crossing by a naval frigate or destroyer.

EXTRACT FROM A DETENTION ORDER MADE BY THE
SECRETARY OF STATE UNDER THE
DEFENCE (GENERAL) REGULATIONS, 1939.

WHEREAS I have reasonable cause to believe the persons mentioned in the schedule to this Order to be persons of hostile associations and that by reason thereof it is necessary to exercise control over them:

NOW, therefore, I in pursuance of the power conferred on me by Regulation 18B of the Defence (General) Regulations, 1939, hereby make the following Order:-

I direct that the persons mentioned in the schedule to this Order be detained.

John Anderson
One of His Majesty's Principal
Secretaries of State.

HOME OFFICE.
WHITEHALL.

~~May, 1940.~~
10th June, 1940.

SCHEDULE.

Ettore EMANUELLI.

The warrant for my arrest under Regulation 18B. Note how the date has been changed from May to June. It looks as though I had been earmarked for an earlier arrest.

ASCOT DAILY SUN (SEMI-OFFICIAL)

Compiled by: L. BIANCHI / E. EMANUELLI B. ROOM

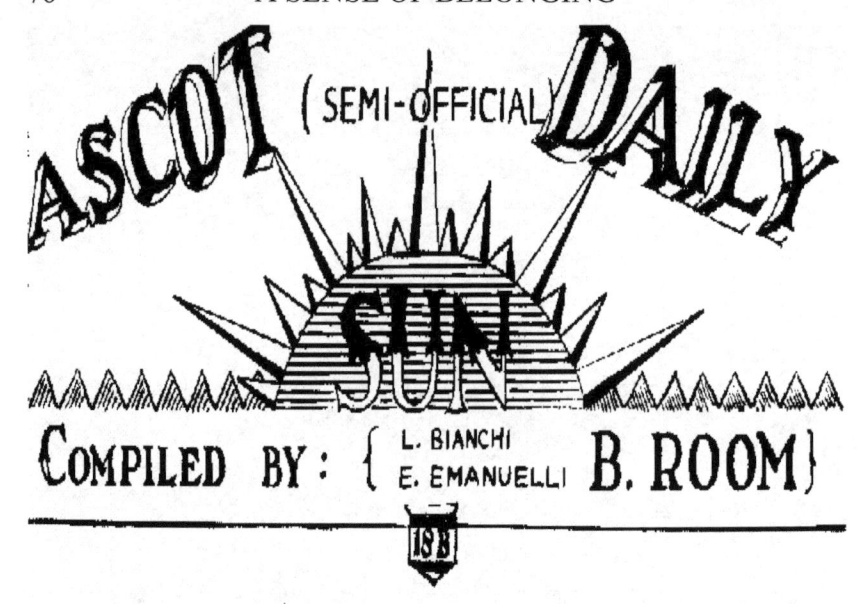

Together with Luigi Bianchi, a fellow detainee from Goole, I tried to launch the 'Ascot Daily Sun' newspaper for the camp. It never got off the ground though.

The Lady of Mann took me to the next camp on the Isle of Man. She had just got back from taking British troops off the beaches at Dunkirk.

CHAPTER 8

Castaway

IN MY SOLITUDE
'A grey-white gull
Majestic, solitary, calling,
A lead-hung sky with night just falling,
A grey-white gull gliding,
To the white laced foam of waves retiring,
A grey-white gull
To thoughts of home inspiring.'
Hector Emanuelli, Peel, 1942

Word had reached the island that a ship-load of dangerous fascists was expected and a hostile crowd had gathered near the landing stage at Douglas. There were boos and shouts from the quay as the Lady of Mann docked. The situation was not helped as the hard-core British fascists on board cheered back provocatively. They also chalked up a slogan on the ship's superstructure: 'MOSLEY FOR PEACE.' The situation threatened to escalate and the authorities decided to keep us on board until the following day when things had quietened down. At six o'clock the next morning, May 13, 1941, we were marched along the North Quay to the railway station, where we boarded a rickety train that took us to the neighbouring town of Peel, where the camp in which we were to be detained was located.

The camp in Peel was referred to as Peveril Camp, or Camp 'M.' I estimate it must have housed some six hundred people. It consisted of a row of large Victorian guesthouses situated at the end of the Promenade near the seawall and of several terraces of smaller houses, all enclosed by barbed wire. The guard rooms and administration offices were situated outside the wire at the nearby Creg Malin Hotel on the Promenade, which the detainees referred to as the Kremlin. Apart from our confinement, conditions were very favourable. We were able to choose with whom we shared a house. Each house was allowed rations for the week and we made our own rotas for cooking and household duties. The camp even had its own currency, printed by the Home Office. Food was short to begin with, but after a while, we began to receive occasional food parcels and mail from our families and friends.

The detainees organised various activities, including football and boxing matches, lectures and language classes. They also swapped books and ran a drama group. People read a lot and took part in discussion groups. Some wrote poetry and painted. Of all the camps, Camp 'M' was the most civilised I had been in, and its inmates were treated humanely. It was in a way almost like a mini-university. I certainly learnt a lot there. The thought of my brother Louis, who was exposed to the very real dangers and discomforts of war, kept me from bemoaning my lot inordinately.

My mother visited me often at the camp. It was quite a journey for her from Stoke. She brought me food parcels when she came. She made friends with the landlady at the guesthouse where she stayed and gave her money to buy things for me. The landlady then sent me parcels now and then. Everything was fair and above board at the camp. All the parcels arrived. Some men received so many parcels they would set up little businesses, bartering the surplus for things they lacked, or they took payment in cigarettes or the camp's currency. I remember I had an Italian tailor from London make me a jacket out of an old army blanket. It turned out very well. I don't remember how I paid him. His name was Rossini and – true to his operatice namesake – he was very musical. He made brave efforts to teach me to play the accordion, sadly in vain!

The second of July 1941 was the first anniversary of the sinking of the Arandora Star. The camp commandant at Peel graciously allowed us to hold a commemorative service outside the wire where we were able to consign a wreath of remembrance into the Irish Sea. I designed a memorial card to accompany a commemorative poem written by fellow detainee, Giulio Sambon.

I used my period of confinement to indulge my love of the theatre, designing posters and sets for revues that the detainees were allowed to put on at the Albert Hall in Peel. One of the shows we staged was 'The Road to Stag-Bad' modelled on the popular 'Road to Singapore' starring Bob Hope, Dorothy Lamour and Bing Crosby, which we had probably seen at the camp cinema. I also had time to try my hand at painting, but having access only to water colours I had no opportunity to make a renewed attempt at reproducing the miner's gloss I had loved as a child in the Rhondda. I did, however, manage to turn out some views of Peel.

I read a lot and wrote some poetry. I dreamt of leaving the family business when I was released and began to hope I might pursue a creative career that was more amenable to my inclinations. Perhaps I could find an opening in the pottery industry back home? How I envied the lot of those renowned ceramic designers from the Potteries – Clarice Cliff, Charlotte Read and Susie Cooper!

Things weren't always quiet in the camp. There were 'disturbances.' On one occasion three men escaped, two Irishmen, members of the IRA, and one member of the British Union of Fascists (BUF). They were soon recaptured, drifting in a boat in the Irish sea. There were unsubstantiated rumours that the men were ill treated after being captured. This triggered riots among the hard-core members of the BUF. They threw everything they could get their hands on at the Creg Malin Hotel, including bricks and toilet seats. No-one was seriously hurt. I kept a very low profile that day!

Eventually, eighteen ringleaders were transferred to Walton Prison in Liverpool, the three escapees ended up in Douglas prison on charges of stealing a boat, and the Metropolitan Police were shipped in to take over from the military, who were relegated to guarding the perimeter. Everything settled down again. The Italians got on very well with the MET. They put together a football team and played against them. They called the team 'Littorio,' which is the name of the fascist symbol. I had no idea what it meant at the time, nor I believe did the boys from the MET. To me it was just a pretty Italian word. I remember doing a poster advertising a game in January 1942. Unfortunately, I don't remember what the score was!

Throughout my detainment I had appeared periodically before various tribunals. I was questioned and cross-examined as to my loyalty to Britain. I had already made unsuccessful appeals before such tribunals in October and December 1940. There was nothing I could say to convince them of my loyalty to King and Country. The hearings were pure Kafka, except that they did not even pretend to be a 'Trial.' They were in fact mere interrogations: no evidence was presented, no reasons given, no witnesses heard. I was completely alone without representation in front of a panel of men who were clearly inimical to me for reasons which they refused to explain. Then, on 13 April 1942, the Camp Commandant in Peel told me that I was to be sent to London to plead my case before another tribunal that was to be held on 17 April, 1942. Letters from my father and mother protesting my innocence finally seemed to have found sympathetic ears. And so it was that I said my farewells to the Isle of Man.

On arrival in Brixton Prison I was assigned to a cell and waited a few days for the hearing. I was cross-examined once more by a panel made up of three men from the MI5. They told me that Father Ryan, my charismatic parish priest back home in Tunstall, had written to the Home Office in May pleading my case. His letter read as follows:

'The Sacred Heart'
Queen's Avenue
Tunstall
Stoke-on-Trent
9th May 1942

To the Undersecretary of State
Home Office London

Dear Sir,

I beg very respectfully to place before you the estimate I hold of the young man – Ettore Emanuelli – who, under Defence of the Realm orders, is now detained in Brixton. I hope it will help towards assuring you that he is not inimical to our British Empire, but, on the contrary, is a genuinely loyal subject, who is ready, and always has been, to serve H. Majesty's interests, either in military or civil capacity as H. Majesty's authority directs. I have known the man's family, and of course the man himself, for many years. They live here now. I have been in constant touch with them. The man's father has been in England for thirty-seven years. In the 1915-'18 war he fought for two years against Germany, and from his attitude, frequently expressed, I gather that he is intensely hostile to the Axis, and honestly loyal to the Allies' cause, and I am convinced that here the son's soul is with his father – that his loyalty to Britain is full and true – this is the conviction that all here, who have known them, hold for the father and son, without exception there is very great sympathy felt for the family, especially for the detained son, the police here are of like conviction on the matter. Ettore did visit Italy in 1939, but I am fully persuaded, the consideration that led to this was the economic advantage of a free pass from England, that enabled him to see his parents' country, of which he had heard, all his life, from them so many great things. His detention is a great sorrow to his parents, and it arises from the feeling that this detention is a stain on their loyalty. They would heartily rejoice to see him enrolled in any form or position in support of the Allied cause. But this suspicion of disloyalty is a constant aching in their lives; and this all the more because they know it is equally bitter to their son. I hope, again with great respect, that you will release him to take the part he yearns to do in the Empire's fight for freedom.

*Respectfully yours
Reverend P. J. Ryan (Catholic Priest)*

The members of the tribunal, or Advisory Committee as it was called, were not impressed, dismissing the letter because Father Ryan was Irish, and hence also of doubtful loyalty! They asked me yet again about that Italian sailor suit and why I had brought it back to the UK. They didn't want to believe it was just a souvenir. I just managed to stop myself from saying "Well, I intended to don it on a dark night, rendezvous with a German submarine, guide it down the Trent and Mersey canal and sink Wedgwood's pot bank.' Thankfully, I restrained myself. They would probably have taken me at my word! Many years later I heard that Anthony Blunt had sat on the Advisory Committee. If this is true it would be the irony of ironies. At that time he was already passing British secrets on to the Russians. A traitor judging the innocent!

I was told my case would be reconsidered and I was taken back to my cell. It was to be a very long time indeed before I heard anything.

I have many memories of my stay in Brixton prison. I was lonelier there than I had been in Peel. One doesn't easily forget the humiliation of 'slopping out', the clanging of cell doors. However, as 'political' detainees we were at least allowed our own clothes and newspapers and we were able to visit other detainees in their cells.

One of the more colourful inmates was the musician Dr Leigh Vaughan Henry. He had been the musical director of the British Union of Fascists. MI5 believed he had developed a notation system through which coded messages could be embedded into pieces of music. He was also suspected of having links with Welsh nationalists. Certainly he had a close association with the Royal Welsh Ladies Choir, whose members, under the leadership of the septuagenarian Welsh singer Clara Novello Davies (mother of Ivor Novello), had planned to dress up as angels and sing for Hitler at the Paris Exhibition of 1937! In 1949 he composed the national anthem of the uninhabited Caribbean island of Redonda ('O God Who Gave Our Island Soil'). Vaughan Henry told me he had been interned by the Germans from 1914 to early 1918, when he had escaped from the Ruhleben camp near Berlin. He had written several poems there which D.H. Lawrence later tried to get published under the title of 'Poems of a Prisoner.' I imagine he must have been more or less my father's age.

One particular recollection often comes back to me: weekly attendance of Sunday mass in the Prison Chapel. Under guard, but separated from the convicts, we saw mass celebrated against the background of a wonderful reredos oil painting worthy of any renaissance church and accompanied by stirring organ music. Sunday was a good day: dinner consisted of corned beef and rice pudding. A true luxury!

Mention of ecclesiastic matters also brings to my mind the occasion when we were visited by an Archbishop, I think it was the Archbishop of Westminster. During the visit, fellow detainee Fredrick Bowman attempted an escape. Bowman was a declared pacifist and an associate of the Duke of Bedford. He had visiting cards printed bearing the motto 'For Peace I Had Great Bitterness' and the address 'Brixton Prison.'

By means I never discovered, he had acquired an Archbishop's robes and by impersonating the visiting archbishop almost got to the main gates before he was rumbled. In civilian life, he was the editor of 'The Talking Picture News.' We would swap newspapers, and he often came to my cell for a chat and to exchange news. Bowman went on hunger strike several times – but once in hospital agreed to take some Marmite and, much to the annoyance of MI5, drank an enormous amount of milk. Very soon after his release, he was involved in an attempt to spring two fellow detainees from captivity. He had planned to kidnap them during a a trip they took outside Brixton to go to the dentists for a regular check-up.

I also recall a certain Giovanni Celeste Sperni, better known as John Sperni, the Mayor of St. Pancras in 1937 and 1938. He was also a justice of the peace, a freemen and a liveryman of the City of London, a prospective London County Council conservative candidate and had twenty-five years of public service behind him. He protested his innocence as a loyal Anglo-Italian and was bitter at being interned under 18b.

In one of her parcels my mother had sent me a large notebook. I used this as a sort of autograph book in which I asked fellow inmates to write a few words. This is why I still remember these people so clearly.

Sadly, during my whole internment I had not received a single letter from Alma. I feared she had forgotten me. But I did receive letters from my parents, my brothers and from Louis' fiancée, Dorina Salvanelli, while I was waiting for the outcome of my review in Brixton. Aldo wrote telling me he had passed his exams and was to go to Form I at Saint Joseph's College after the holidays. Louis wrote telling me he was safe and was posted temporarily at Bournemouth.

Perhaps it was the kind intercession on Father Ryan's part after all that finally convinced the authorities of my innocence. At any rate, after five long months of deliberation the Advisory Committee found in my favour and on 11 August I was notified that I was to be released from Brixton Prison. The following morning I ventured out into the bustling city of London, completely disoriented and bewildered.

I made my way to Euston Station and caught a train to Stoke-on-Trent. Josiah Wedgwood's statue outside Stoke Station looked pleased to see me again! My parents were overjoyed to have me home at last.

Outside the boarding house in Peel where I was interned. I'm standing next to the man with the accordion – Dominic Rea from Ancoats Little Italy in Manchester.

86 A SENSE OF BELONGING

Camp M's Anglo-Italian football team. Winter 1941/2. See next page for the names of the players.

FOOTBALL MATCH

TUES. 13TH JAN.
KICK OFF 2-30.

LITTORIO
v.
MET. POLICE

Littorio	Met. Police
Bertolini	Best
Giorgi Capaldi	Fryer Bosley
Donfrancesco Chiesa Azzario	Pyke Sharpe King
Romana Donfrancesco Bessolo	Wood Minns Carter
Pacitti Mancini	Simper Vicars

REF. P.C. PHILIPS

Linesman - Cocozza.   Linesman. Ferrari.

The match between the Italian and MET teams held on 13 January 1942.

Fellow detainees at Peveril Camp in Peel in 1941. I'm third from the right in the front row.

Notturno: Un'impressione.

One of my watercolour paintings of Saint Patrick's Isle, Peel. 1942.

I had a lot of fun designing the sets for this show. I did the poster, too.

Castaway 91

setting from "THE ROAD TO STAG-BAD" designed by ettore emanuelli

Fellow detainee Leigh Vaughan Henry drew this for me in my autograph book. It shows his home in Ewell.

Castaway

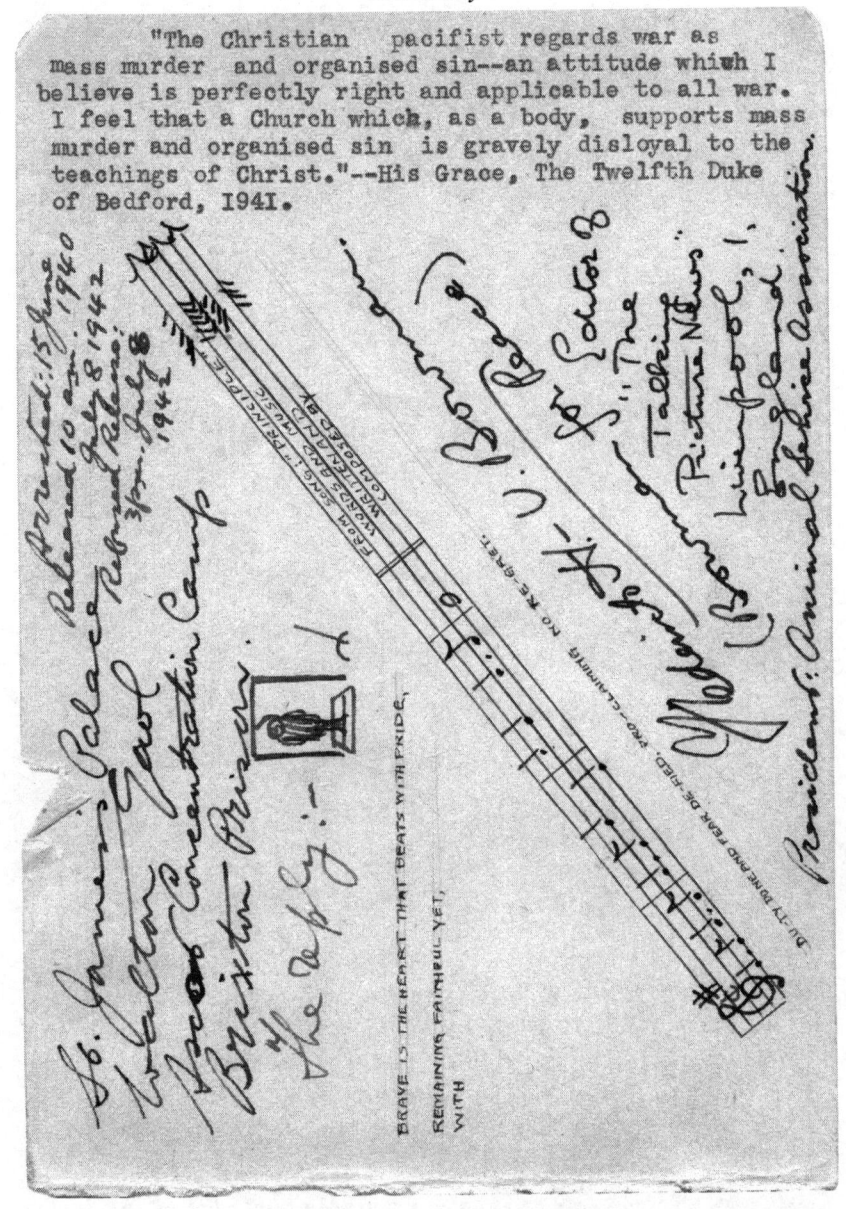

> "The Christian pacifist regards war as mass murder and organised sin—an attitude which I believe is perfectly right and applicable to all war. I feel that a Church which, as a body, supports mass murder and organised sin is gravely disloyal to the teachings of Christ."—His Grace, The Twelfth Duke of Bedford, 1941.

Pacifist H.- U. Bowman wrote this for me. Note the quote from the 12th Duke of Bedford.

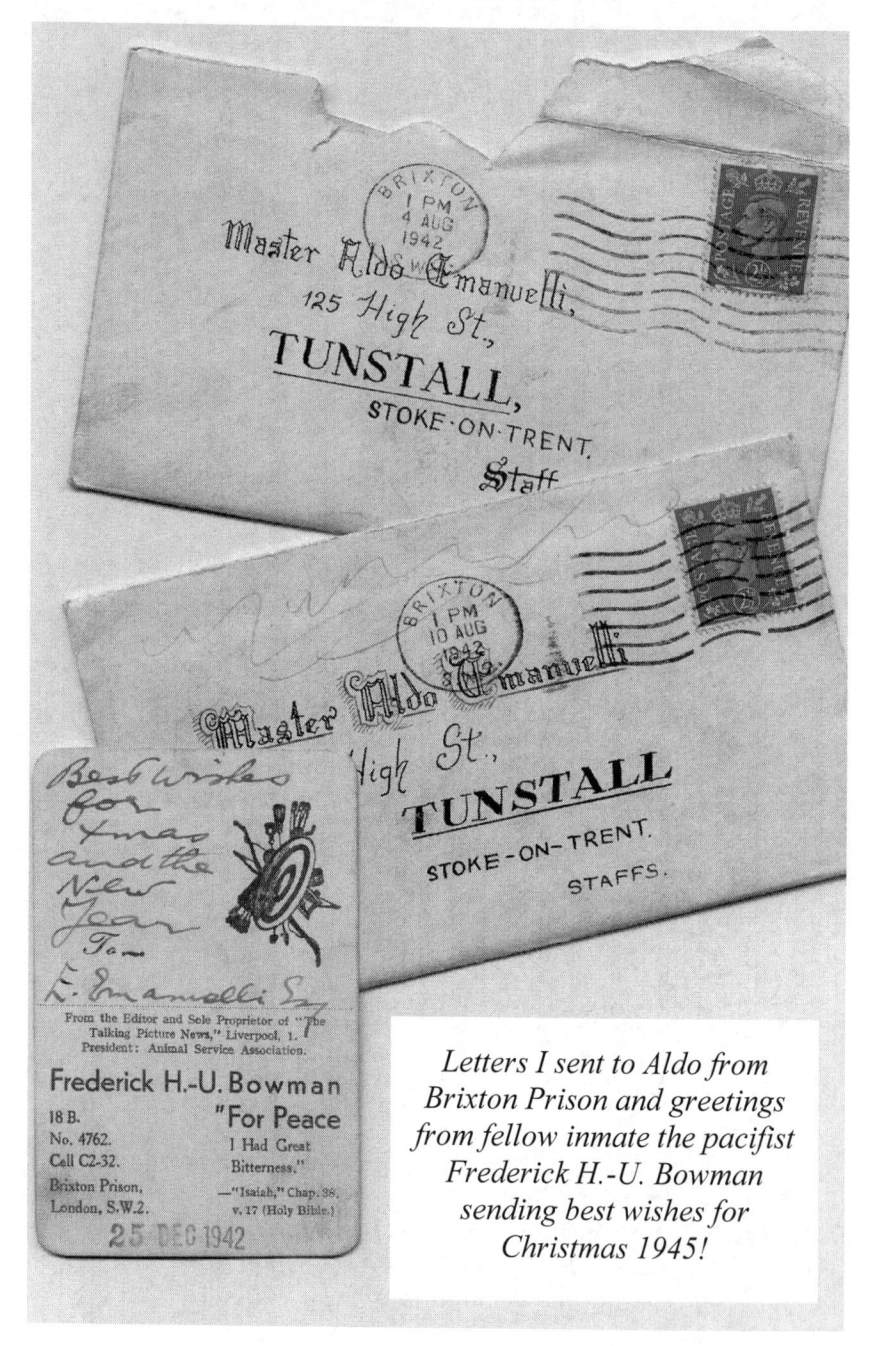

Letters I sent to Aldo from Brixton Prison and greetings from fellow inmate the pacifist Frederick H.-U. Bowman sending best wishes for Christmas 1945!

* Any communication on the subject of this letter should be addressed to—
THE UNDER SECRETARY OF STATE,
HOME OFFICE, LONDON, S.W.1.
and the following number quoted:—

840025/7

Your Ref.

G.2 Division,
HOME OFFICE,
WHITEHALL.

11th August, 1942

Sir,

    I am directed by the Secretary of State to inform you that he has reviewed your case again in the light of all the circumstances and has directed under Regulation 18B(2) of the Defence (General) Regulations, 1939, that the operation of the Order for your detention shall be suspended. A copy of the Direction has been handed to you.

        I am,
        Sir,
    Your obedient Servant,

W. Lyon

E. Emanuelli, Esq.,

Finally! The letter handed to me on 11 August 1942 informing me of my impending release.

96   A SENSE OF BELONGING

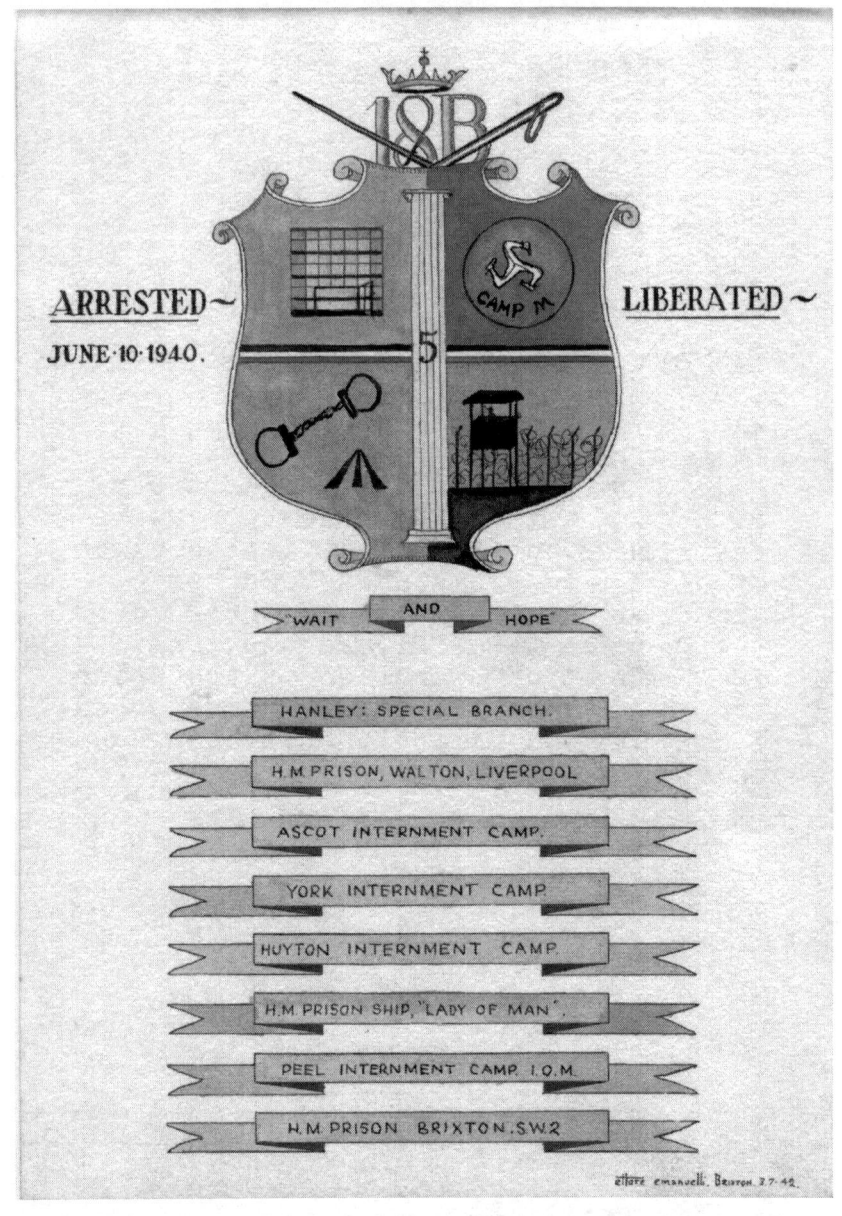

'Wait & Hope.' I did this in July 1942 in Brixton Prison to pass the time while waiting for the Advisory Committee to decide on my fate. They finally released me on 11 August, 1942.

CHAPTER 9

Directed Labour

*'Solo e pensoso i più deserti campi
vo mesurando a passi tardi e lenti,
e gli occhi porto per fuggir intenti
ove vestigio uman l'arena stampi.'**
Franceso Petrarca, Rime Sparse

After over two years of confinement I was a nervous wreck. I felt that all eyes were on me and that I was completely abandoned and isolated. For a while, I even wished that I was back on the Isle of Man with the friends I had made there and who had cried for me when I left the camp. Nor did I feel that my release had been a complete exoneration. I still felt branded as an outsider.

The authorities had told me I would be contacted in due course by the local Labour Exchange, who would allocate me to suitable employment. In the meantime, I was to report to the local police station. I was still not a truly free man.

From my release in August I remained in limbo until the Burslem Employment Exchange finally contacted me early

---

* Alone and lost in thought
I pace out lonesome fields
with a slow and measured step,
ready to cast down my eyes
where others pass.

February 1943. I reported to their offices in Ward Street. I told them I wished to join the armed forces, preferably the Royal Air Force! After all, my brother Louis had fought in the Norwegian campaign and was now serving in the British Eighth Army in North Africa.

The manager of the Labour Exchange, with a look of complete disdain and with a sarcastic tone of voice, said 'You will certainly not be accepted in H.M. Forces. I am directed to inform you that you are to be the subject of a Directed Labour Order.' Picking up a slip of paper from his desk, he read aloud. 'You shall therefore be required to report to the Arden and Cobden Hotel Group in Birmingham, where you will take up the position of waiter at a wage of three pounds a week, live-in, all found.' And so it seemed to me I was no longer to be master of my own destiny. My detention order was merely 'suspended,' not rescinded, and I was to be 'directed.'

As 'directed,' I turned up at the Cobden Hotel on the appointed date of February 12, 1943, to be told they had no need of a waiter and that I should report to the Arden Hotel in New Street, next to the Odeon Cinema. I found the hotel easily enough. To have called it a four-star establishment would be a great exaggeration. But with its convenient location in relation to the New Street Railway Station and the Corporation Street shopping attractions one could with some honesty give it at least two stars. In reality, it was purely a commercial hotel catering for travelling salesmen and shoppers, and served as a stop-over for ongoing travellers.

On my arrival there to report for duty I was met by a surly-tempered individual who tried to foster the impression that he was either the Hotel Manager or even the owner. He turned out to be the Hall Porter. I took an instant dislike to him. In his self-importance, he reminded me of Ex-Sergeant-Major Buck from Warwick Deeping's 'Sorrell and Son.' He reluctantly introduced me to the manageress, a nondescript lady of medium height, bespectacled, wispy-haired, who appeared to be completely under his domination. I introduced myself and she explained that I was required to work as 'second chef' under the supervision of a certain Chef Coda.

She also told me that while I was so employed I would be referred to by the name of 'Tony.' This was the name that all second chefs at the hotel had always been assigned! So even my name was to be taken from me, but I raised no objections, I simply added it to the growing list of aliases I had been known by so far in my life; Torino, Ettorino, Etto, Ettore, and the anglicised Hector that I had acquired when I attended the King Edward VI Grammar School in Stratford-upon-Avon.

I was soon accepted by the rest of the staff, who – like myself – were all objects of Directed Labour.

We were a motley crew at the hotel. Most of the waitresses were Irish. They included two sisters, Margaret and Mary, who were distinct opposites. Margaret was tall, very serious and deeply religious. Her sister Mary was very gregarious and full of fun. Helga the Austrian was small and of indeterminate age, very polite and efficient. Then there was another Irish girl, Florrie. She spoke with a wonderful brogue and had flaming red hair. Although her name was Florrie French, there was certainly nothing French about Florrie! She was pure and unadulterated Irish, and gloriously so. For some reason Florrie had taken a shine to me.

The waitresses were under the orders of the diminutive and cross-eyed Head Waiter. The waitresses would refer to him as Napoleon behind his back. Personally, I saw little resemblance with the Corsican.

My duties included serving on the 'Still Room Hot Plate' as the waitresses came in with their orders at lunch and dinner times. I got on well with them and would often accompany them to their Irish dances at Handsworth when I was off duty. Florrie flirted furiously with me!

The hotel kitchen was a domain for itself. It was located in the hotel basement. There was no daylight. It was very hot and had no ventilation. It certainly would not have complied with today's stringent food regulations or current heath-and-safety requirements.

Under Chef Coda's directions we worked wonders even under such dire circumstances. Mrs. Dunphy, the pastry cook, a sullen lady who seldom spoke but got on with her work, turned out tarts and pastries that were much to Chef Coda's satisfaction. Mrs Edwards was the vegetable cook, small and busy, continually circulating around her pots and exchanging the odd ribald remark with the kitchen porter, then muttering to herself, for all the world like some witch hovering around her beloved cauldron.

Supplies were naturally short in 1943. Chicken, for example, was very hard to come by. But we had a steady supply of rabbit that was being shipped in from Ireland. Unfortunately, rabbit was not very popular with diners. No problem for Chef Coda. What came into his kitchen as Irish rabbit left it transmuted into 'Chicken Cutlets à la Coda.' I don't think anyone complained!

Helping out Chef Coda was not my only duty at the hotel. Once a week I was also the Fire Watcher up on the roof of the hotel. I would spend all evening scanning the surroundings for fires caused by German bombing. After London and Liverpool, Birmingham was the third most heavily bombed city in Britain. The last raids occurred in April 1943. Fire-watching leaves you a lot of time to think, and it was while sitting on the roof of the Arden Hotel that I composed this 'anti-war' poem:

Is this world indeed possessed
By some satanic quest,
Venting its fury without respite,
Descending with death upon the night?
Is there no justice upon this earth,
No truth or love to welcome our birth?
Why do we fight and bomb and kill,
Murdering our brothers against our will?
Has this world indeed gone mad,
Stirred by some new political fad
Uniting with Satan to rape and win
Plunging our souls into a life of sin?

Where is the right, the will to live,
If we only take and never give?
Why do we continue to war and hate,
Exulting in death and stormy debate?
We grope in a world of darkness and doubt,
Perishing souls in a nightmare drought.
Just living to kill, to drink red blood,
Drowning all peace in a devilish flood.
God give us strength to see the light.
Makes us see right to crush this might.
Teach all men the meaning of war.
Teach all to love and obey your law.
God give our souls that yearning for peace
Then perhaps once more we shall find release
From this tempest of wrath and bloody fires
Fed from the skies by those uniformed fliers.
God teach us once more the way to live,
Never to hate, but to love and to forgive!

Like myself, Chef Coda had also been 'directed' to work in Birmingham. He was in fact an Italian cockney and a highly-paid London chef who had been commended by and received medals from Queen Mary. We got on very well together. He treated me like a son. During slack periods, usually in the afternoons, he would say to me: 'Come on Tony – let's go and have a hair cut!' He would make an appointment at some rather expensive salon and – after luxuriating there for awhile – would return to the hotel just in time to make preparations for the evening dinner guests.

I shared accommodation with Chef Coda at the company's house at Handsworth, where he lived with his wife Maria, his daughter Connie and his young son Frank. I would often accompany young Frank to New Street Station where I saw him onto his train to Tamworth, where he attended a private school.

As it happened, Chef Coda was an amateur artist and we would often discuss painting. We also painted together in the evenings after work. He had a good supply of oil paints which he let me use and under his expert guidance for the first time I was able to try and get that 'miner's gloss' that had so impressed me when I was a boy in the Rhondda. My first subject was a portrait of my childhood sweetheart, Alma Carpanini. Chef Coda devoted his time to emulating the French impressionists. He was a great man and I learnt a lot from him, both as a painter and also in the field of the culinary arts, which was to benefit me greatly later on in the family business. As soon as I had finished the portrait of Alma, I sent it to her in South Wales and looked forward to hearing her opinion of it.

I was to a certain extent happy and enjoying the company of Chef Coda, his family and the friends I had made at the hotel. All the same, I felt like a fish out of water in Birmingham. I felt as though I were in exile. A foreigner in my own country. I was anxious to return to Tunstall, where before the war I had started to feel I belonged.

Thankfully, I had every second weekend off. This allowed me to go home to Tunstall. Rationing continued to make business difficult. It's hard to make ice cream without milk. Fortunately, by now the Americans had arrived! This may have been viewed as a mixed blessing by some, as the 'over-paid, over-sexed, and over HERE!' joke reflects, but for my parents it was a true boon: among the GIs posted in Staffordshire were several Italo-Americans. Somehow they had discovered the 'Wonder Bar' and the fact that it was run by Italians. The US soldiers had lots of money, lots of time – at least until the D-Day landings – and a great appetite for Italian food. Most important – they had lots of supplies and provisions! They seemed to be able to get hold of anything. Shrewd as ever, my mother was quick to understand this. Before long she was spoiling them! With the flour they brought her she made them endless plates of pastasciutta served with her marvellous ragù Bolognese and ravioli in brodo. With the eggs, sugar and Marsala wine they supplied she conjured up dishes of her beautiful *zambaion' alla paesana,* which – unlike the more refined *zabaione* you might get in an Italian restaurant these days – was firm and rich and had so much Marsala in it that it was mildly intoxicating. In return for the cooking, the US soldiers would supply large tubs of powdered milk that had fallen off the back of the quartermaster's truck back at base. My father had realised that this was an ideal ingredient for ice-cream making. His production started to soar again!

This was a perfect Anglo-American symbiosis! I loved it when these Americans were there during my fortnightly weekend visits to Tunstall. True, they were big, noisy and brash, but relaxed, hearty and sincere. They called my father 'Pop' just like the Godfather's sons call Marlon Brando in the film of the same name. From then on my father was always known as Pop, and somehow it suited him as he rounded out in middle-age.

During my period of detainment on the Isle of Man, in Brixton Prison and now during my sojourn at the Arden Hotel, I had hatched many plans in my head on how to expand the family business when I was released. Now I was longing to get away from Birmingham and back to Tunstall to put these plans into practice.

Back in 1940, when I had first been detained and sent to Walton Prison, I had been given a cursory medical examination. I had never been told so explicitly, but the identifying card displayed outside my prison cell which read 'No Lifting!' actually meant I had a hernia. I had never had any trouble with the hernia, but given the circumstances I thought that this would be a good time to have it seen to.

Confiding my intentions to Chef Coda, he agreed that I should seek medical advice and suggested that I try to get leave of absence in order to have an operation. In the meantime, I had consulted my own doctor, who had no objection to issuing the required certificate. Armed with this and bypassing the dreaded Hall Porter, I approached Miss Lewis the Manageress. After some persuasion, she agreed that I should have time off for treatment. When the time came for me to go to hospital towards the end of 1943, she wished me well, adding the words 'we shall all miss you very much, Tony. Now do be sure to come back fit and well.'

I was admitted to the Haywood Hospital in Burslem, not far from home, which meant my family could visit me. The operation went well, but in those days convalescence was long. During the second week of my stay at the Haywood, I received an unexpected visit from Florrie, the red-haired Irish colleen who had flirted with me at the Arden Hotel. Disregarding hospital visiting hours, she burst into Ward 9 with a flourish. She had obviously by-passed the sister in charge or she may well have exerted her considerable Irish charms to gain admission. Plumping herself on the bed, her elegant legs dangling, in her lilting Irish brogue she exclaimed – 'Ah Tony me love, how're ye keeping? To be sure now we all miss you at the hotel.' She went on to give me all the news from the kitchen to the stillroom and the latest gossip about the head waiter and the waitresses. My fellow patients were agog, their eyes wide with amazement, and I'm sure that their temperatures must have leapt several degrees. I was a little embarrassed by Florrie's scenes of endearment and rather relieved when she said that sadly she would have to leave to catch her train back to Birmingham. She was on duty that evening. It was very good of her to sacrifice her day off to visit me, but I had no romantic feelings towards her – after all I was still carrying a torch for my childhood sweetheart Alma Carpanini.

I was well looked after while I was in hospital, especially by a certain Student Nurse Hulse. There were six patients in our ward and whenever Student Nurse Hulse did the rounds, bringing fresh water to our bedside tables, my cup always appeared to be the nicest. Was this preferential treatment? I hoped it was. Student Nurse Hulse was very pretty!

When I came out of hospital in 1943 I was still not considered fit to return to work in Birmingham. After a while I was informed that the Directed Labour Order had lapsed and I was free to return to the family business. My time at the Arden Hotel, where I had made such good friends, had come to an end. Sadly, I was never to see the hotel again. On a recent visit to Birmingham I noted that it had been demolished to make way for the Bull Ring. Nor was I ever to see Chef Coda or the flirtatious Florrie French again.

The Arden Hotel in a post-war advertisement. Naturally, the Wimpy Bar and the skyscraper weren't there in 1943 and the Odeon Cinema looked quiet different.

Aldo at the front on the left with three waitresses from the Wonder Bar in the early 1940s. Note the American-style soda jerk uniforms. We had learned a lot from the GIs. Also in the picture a confectionery bag from the Wonder Bar.

The Carpanini Sisters. Alma on the accordion, Irene on the tambourine. Alma was my childhood sweetheart.

'Pop' outside the Wonder Bar in Tunstall. He got his new name from the American GIs stationed around Stoke.

CHAPTER 10

Building the Business

'So this was business! It was not the business he desired and meant to have; and he was uneasy at the extent to which he was already entangled in it; but it was rather amusing ....'
Arnold Bennett, Clayhanger

In summer 1943, like a bolt out of the blue I received the news that Alma had married. Although she had hardly written to me since I had last seen her in 1939, she had remained very much in my thoughts, a distant, unreachable Petrarchan Laura! I suppose I had been in love with being in love. All the same, in my fragile mental state after years of detention and directed labour, I was frankly shaken when I heard that she had married. No wonder she had not acknowledged receipt of the portrait I had painted of her! Perhaps it is still mouldering to this day in some attic in South Wales. I fell into a deep depression.

My parents convinced me to take a holiday in Rhyl. My brother Aldo came with me. The sea air and Aldo's company helped a lot. I took stock of my position. The girl I had dreamt would one day be my wife had married another man. My morale was dented by my detention in internment camps and prisons and the stain it had left on my name. I was denied an opportunity to fight for my country. I saw no hope of embarking on the creative career I had dreamt of during my internment. I was almost twenty-three years old and I had few formal school qualifications. Before the war things had looked so good, but for the past three years they had been so bleak. I took some solace in the thought that I had my family, who had always stood by me. I returned to Tunstall somewhat restored. Though the future looked grim, I steeled myself to work hard and make the best of a bad job.

At the end of July came the news that Mussolini had been arrested, in September the Italians surrendered to the Allies and by mid-October they had declared war on their former ally. This was very good news for the Italians in England and Wales. They were now no longer regarded as potential enemies. The winter came and went, and Louis was still part of the allies' 'slow slog' up the Italian peninsula. We were all very anxious for him. History repeats itself. Like his father twenty-six years earlier in the First World War, Louis too was driving a military truck. By the spring of 1944 he was billeted at Teano, half way between Naples and Rome and some sixty kilometres to the south of Monte Cassino. He must have made a great and lasting impression: when he returned after the war he received postcards and letters from the family he had been billeted with. They were signed 'Your little sisters, Antonietta, Ellena, Nicolina, and Lilina!'

The war ground on. Rome was finally freed in early June. The allies fought their way very slowly up the peninsula. *Partigiani* were fighting in the hills around Bardi, unleashing a campaign of reprisals by the Nazis and fascists in which many perished. The local people hid British airmen and prisoners of war who had escaped from Fontanellato and other camps back in 1943 when Mussolini had fallen. The Nazis and fascists made frequent raids, combing the hills for escapees. In July 1944, my paternal grandfather's village of Cereseto was burnt to the ground by German soldiers and fascists as a reprisal for partisan attacks. Three civilians were shot. Even worse atrocities occurred in other villages.

Then at last Germany surrendered and the hostilities were over. After the joyous VE-Day celebrations in May the world began to return to normality. We all hoped Louis would be home soon. Father's rotor arm had been returned and his dove-grey Hillman Minx was back on the road. To celebrate the car's resurrection, I took a trip down to Treherbert and visited old friends. Among others, I visited the Salvanelli family. Mrs. Salvanelli had been a friend of my mother way back when they had been girls together in Bardi. Her two charming daughters, Dorina – Louis' fiancée – and Gloria, were there when I visited. It was of course painful to be in the Rhondda and not be able to visit Alma, but she was by now a married woman and it would have been even more painful for me if I had seen her.

Italian families in South Wales were in mourning for the fathers, sons and brothers they had lost on the Arandora star. Many familiar names were among the dead: Antoniazzi, Basini, Belli, Carpanini, Conti, Ferrari, Franchi, Fulgoni, Gazzi, Lusardi, Marenghi, Moruzzi, Rabaiotti, Ricci, Rossi, Sidoli, Solari, Sterlini, Strinati, Taffurelli, Zanelli, Zanetti. The mood among the Italians in the valleys was depressed, but the few Italian cafes that were left continued trading.

Back in Tunstall, business at our Wonder Bar in the High Street was beginning to pick up again. It had become very popular with young girls and boys, who would congregate there in the evenings and at weekends, simply chatting or planning a holiday at a Butlin's Holiday Camp or some such place. There was never any trouble and even today some sixty-five years later people who were customers at that time come up to me and reminisce about those 'good old days.'

It was at the Wonder Bar that we first introduced our young clientele to such delights as the Knickerbocker Glory, the Banana Split, the Peach Melba, the Chocolate Nut Sundae and the Mars Bar Sundae. We may well have been the first to incorporate a famous chocolate bar into an ice cream. We were in fact applauded by the Mars Company for this enterprise. We also got some inspiration from those US GIs. We kitted our staff out in American-style soda jerk uniforms.

The church played a large part in my life. In my constant search for a sense of belonging I had joined the Knights of St.

Columba, a Catholic lay society that organised charitable events and supported the local clergy. I was made very welcome. We met monthly in the Neo-Romanesque crypt of Father Ryan's 'Sacred Heart Church.' It was great fun. We wore sashes, medals and other regalia and followed strict rituals and had passwords and signs. Within the society's hierarchy of Supreme and Grand Knights and Brothers of the Order, I occupied the not insignificant position of Recorder, which meant I kept the minutes of the meetings we held. Later, I was promoted to the status of Inquisitor, whose role it was to initiate new members into the Order's rituals. This took place in the Church of St. Peter at Cobridge. I must admit I loved it!

One day at the Wonder Bar I noticed a familiar face among the customers. It was Student Nurse Hulse. She was as pretty as ever. Engaging her in conversation, I found out her first name was Joan. It turned out that she lived in Goldenhill, just up the road from Tunstall, and also came from a Catholic family. I plucked up all my courage and invited her to the cinema. She said yes. The beginning of a new romance, I hoped. We were not able to see each other very often as she was still nursing at the Haywood Hospital and often found it difficult getting time off, but soon you could say that we were 'courting.'

In the meantime, demand for our ice-cream started to recover, the cafe's capacity was beginning to become overstretched again. We needed larger premises, both for the cafe trade and also for ice-cream production. We bought another shop further down the High Street. The plan was to open an additional cafe to cater for the morning coffee trade, serving lunch-time meals and afternoon teas as well as attracting the evening and week-end trade, with our faithful teenage customers continuing to make use of the friendly setting at the Wonder Bar.

The launch of the new cafe kept my parents, Aldo and I very busy through 1946 and 1947. My brother Louis had still not returned from the forces. There were interminable meetings with the licensing authorities and sanitary and food inspectors. There seemed to be no end to the permits required, right down to the 'Performing Rights' permit that would allow us to play music in the cafe. Decisions had to be made regarding the layout and fittings for the interior. The furniture, crockery, light fittings and kitchen equipment had to be ordered. Waitresses had to be interviewed, a chef engaged. Builders and decorators were involved, and for a time it seemed that the new cafe would never materialise.

My mother had undertaken the interior decoration and engaged the local firm of Leon M. Rowe to carry out the work. Her inspiration came from the decor of the Odeon Cinema in Hanley, which she had always admired. I had designed the fascia with the logo of the cafe in lower case lettering on black glass in the art deco style. The logo was also used on the front door, while the Hanley-based firm of Louis di Ceccho also used it for the terrazzo floor that they laid out for the cafe's doorstep.

The 'Castle Bardi' windows were a major feature of the interior. These depicted Bardi Castle and the bridge over the river Ceno. I had commissioned the firm of Weirs Glass to produce these in stained glass. They were back-lit from the kitchen and were a focal point for guests in the restaurant.

I recall an occasion when the legendary Father Ryan paid a visit to the cafe: I asked him, 'Father, what do you think of our stained-glass windows?' He put his hand on my shoulder, and looking at me with his good eye (his other eye was glass), he said to me 'To be sure my son, those are leaded lights, not stained glass.' I did not argue with him, after all he had scoured Europe for artistic embellishments for the magnificent Sacred Heart church he had built in Tunstall and he obviously knew his stuff as far as stained glass was concerned. One never argued with Father Ryan, anyway. But to me they were stained glass, and I was very proud of them.

The new cafe finally opened in autumn 1947. We called it the Cafe Continental. The February 1948 edition of the trade magazine 'Ice Cream Topics' sang its praises as follows:

'ELEGANCE IN THE MIDLANDS
A Really Artistic Establishment

Messrs. Emanuel & Sons' Cafe Continental in High Street, Tunstall, Staffs, is one of those rare establishments one hardly hopes to meet in industrial surroundings. A veritable oasis in a desert, as a traveller described it; an eye opener.

It was obviously not planned and opened in a day: if anything, it took two whole years to secure licences and goods, materials, equipment, etc. Many years of intensive trading in South Wales had taught the family the trend of things, and what was the best; they were determined to secure it at all costs. Everything was carefully and painstakingly planned, from the gorgeous shop front fascia and windows, to counter, shelves, lighting system, etc., not to mention fittings, silverware and service. This last, allied to quality, is the family motto.

The internal colour scheme is in perfect tone with the firm's trade colours – orange and cream. The dado is maroon, finished in a Japanese leather effect. The walls are in tangerine, stippled in gold. A gold band edged with green runs round the entire cafe.

The shopping hall counter, and buffet bars, are in green and cream – a delightful combination, forming a perfect background for the waitresses' uniforms in tangerine and chocolate. No expense was spared in the matter of counter fittings, showcases, silverware and glassware, napery, tablecloths, menus, etc. London's West End at its best, was the goal aimed at, to be surpassed if anything, especially in individual service and utmost elegance.

The elegant menus are printed in gold, chocolate and orange, and enumerate some 60 items from the many served. Ice cream, the firm's speciality, is given the centre of page 3, thus catching the customer's eye immediately. Vanilla, Strawberry or College Ices are listed at 6d.; Strawberry or Chocolate Sundaes, Banana Split or Snow White Sundaes at 9d.; Apricot Louise or Peach Melba at 1s. and 1s. 6d. respectively.

Building the Business

There are 9 Cold Drinks, from 5d. to 8d., the latter including Ice Cream Sodas, and 9 Hot Beverages from 4d. to 6d. Cold meats and salads, including Chicken Salad, range from 1s. to 2s. 6d., while the restaurant lines, such as Hot Dishes, are listed at 10d. to 1s. 6d. There are a dozen of each of the last two groups.

The back of the menus is given over to a description of the two stained glass windows at the rear of the counter; real works of art designed and executed by Weir's (Glass) Ltd., of Hanley. They represent Castle Bardi and its beautiful countryside in the province of Parma, Northern Italy, the home of many successful caterers and ice-cream traders operating in Britain, America, etc. Much havoc was deliberately done there by the German forces and S.S. during the recent war, because the men and women were pro-British and formed themselves into a veritable stronghold for resistance, partisan units, etc. Those who were not captured and sent to forced labour in Germany, hid in the hills and woods, hindering the Germans as much as possible. The London B.B.C. was contacted for nightly instructions, while our R.A.F. dropped food supplies and ammunition, and picked up escaped airmen and soldiers, fed and hidden by the Bardi partisans. Bardi is always saluted with dipped wings by R.A.F. aircraft, in memory of much valour and help, and of the villages and homesteads deliberately burnt and destroyed by the baulked Germans, who just hated to have to retreat after so many actual or apparent victories. They forgot to destroy the souls of the local inhabitants: the places have been rebuilt and all is activity there once more.

Famous Ice Cream

The firm's original establishment at N° 125 High Street, is now their ice-cream factory, modern, hygienic and fully equipped. Emanuellis' smooth and perfectly balanced ice cream is not only served in their Cafe Continental, *but also in local cinemas, cafes, confectioners, etc. Wrapped bars and cartons have proved a huge success, and they now find that the Family Block is forging ahead remarkably well – quite the line of the future. Our readers will remember that, in America, the Family Brick, Week-End Brick, Sunday Brick, etc. shot up sales and remained to stay, a constant advertisement for the supplier's ice cream, and always prompting more.*

The head of the firm is Mr. G. Emanuelli, far from old in activity, although many years have passed since he started in the ice-cream and refreshment trade at the age of 15. His son Ettore is general manager, organiser in chief and, incidentally, the designer of the shop front, fixtures, fittings, etc.; Louis is production manager, very jealous of the ice-cream factory and the good name of the daily product. But question these three, and they parry all compliments, assuring all and sundry that it is dear old Mrs. Emanuelli who really keeps things going smoothly, working and smiling all the day long. The trade should be proud of them all, and, no doubt is. It is surely a case of enterprise rewarded.'

Achille Pompa, Ice Cream Topics, February 1948

So things were looking up again. All the hard work and frustration had borne fruit and our new enterprise was turning out to be a great success. But we did not intend to rest on our laurels. We had yet more plans in store!

In 1943, broken-hearted after my childhood sweetheart married another man, I took a break in Rhyl. Aldo came to keep me company. Louis in uniform. He'd already fought in the Norwegian Campaign and North Africa, and in 1944 he saw action in Italy.

Student Nurse Joan Hulse receiving her nursing certificate. She brought the sunshine back into my life.

The Cafe Continental, 1948. I designed the fascia with the logo of the cafe in lower case lettering on black glass in the art deco style. The logo was also used on the front door, while the Hanley-based firm of Louis di Ceccho used it for the terrazzo floor that they laid out for the cafe's doorstep.

The interior of the Cafe Continental with the Castle Bardi windows at the back.

cafe continental

TUNSTALL

EMANUEL & SONS, 179 HIGH STREET, TUNSTALL

'The elegant menus are printed in gold, chocolate and orange, and enumerate some 60 items from the many served. Ice cream, the firm's speciality, is given the centre of page 3, thus catching the customer's eye immediately. Vanilla, Strawberry or College Ices are listed at 6d.; Strawberry or Chocolate Sundaes, Banana Split or Snow White Sundaes at 9d.; Apricot Louise or Peach Melba at 1s. and 1s. 6d. respectively.'

Courting!

CHAPTER 11

Tying the Knot

'In the Five Towns, and perhaps elsewhere, there exists a custom in virtue of which a couple who have become engaged in the early summer find themselves by a most curious coincidence at the same seaside resort, and often in the same street thereof, in August.' Arnold Bennett, The Card

By 1947 I had recovered greatly from my war-time depression. I was feeling stronger and more self-confident. So much so, in fact, that I was able to gather enough courage to propose to Joan. She said yes. So now we were really a couple. I was very proud of her. She was a true English rose, very pretty, elegant and refined. After the nightmare of detention and the pain of rejection, I began to feel that I fitted in again and was accepted.

The launch of the Cafe Continental had taken its toll on me and now that it was up and running I was exhausted. I was very stressed and losing weight. My parents insisted that I spend a week-long recuperating by the seaside, and Joan was to come with me, they said. And so it was that I arranged that we spend a week at Blackpool.

We stayed at the Danum Hotel on the quieter south shore of Blackpool. In case you're wondering, we stayed in separate rooms! The hotel was owned by Alderman G.L. Barber, the famous patron of a handful of cinemas in the Potteries, which we were already supplying with our ice cream. This was a big customer. His younger brother Albert was also staying at the same hotel so I still found myself talking business. We all enjoyed each other's company as we relaxed in the bracing sea breezes at Blackpool. Joan and I planned our wedding. We pencilled it in for autumn of the following year.

Finally, in 1948, Louis returned from the forces. Mother and father together with my younger brother Aldo took over the running of the cafes in Tunstall, while Louis and I dedicated ourselves to the next project. Our ice-cream production capacity in Tunstall was stretched to the limit, business was booming and we were unable to meet the growing demand. The solution? Louis and I set about searching for premises where we could open a new and modern ice-cream factory with all the latest equipment and sufficient capacity to satisfy demand.

Louis and Dorina Salvanelli had been courting for some time now and were planning to marry shortly after Joan and I. This distracted us somewhat from our plans for an ice-cream factory, which we put on ice for a while, if you'll excuse the pun.

For some months prior to the wedding Joan and I had been thinking about where we should go for our honeymoon. Of course there was no question in my mind: it would have to be Italy! Joan agreed. In 1948, however, there was no such thing as a 'package holiday' so we paid a visit to the Hanley offices of Thomas Cook & Son. We gave them our instructions for what was to be our 'Grand Tour,' starting in Rome and taking in the Vatican, Florence, Fiesole, San Marino, Pisa, and Genoa on the Ligurian coast. The last stage of the honeymoon was, of course, to be spent in Bardi, where I hoped to introduce my English Rose to my Italian relatives and the tranquil, rural life of the northern Apennines.

The day of our wedding was suddenly upon us. I was a bag of nerves! As a wedding gift, I had bought Joan a pair of fire opals and diamond drop earrings, and she had bought me a pair of golden cuff links. Louis' surprise gift to both Joan and myself was to arrange a cine-film of the wedding. This was shot by Martin's of Hanley. With the bright film lights and the sound of the camera we felt just a little like movie stars!

Nuptial Mass was not performed very often at Goldenhill and the parish priest Father O'Connor took the opportunity of inviting the whole of the junior school to witness the ceremony. Joan and I were unaware of this at the time. The church was filled to capacity and as Joan walked down the aisle on her father's arm a lump came into my throat. She looked the complete 'English Rose' and I felt ten feet tall!

The reception was held at the George Hotel in Burslem, with one hundred guests from England, Wales and Italy. The top table was decorated with a giant four-tier wedding cake. I guess that someone in the family had pulled some strings with the caterers Frank L. Swynnerton and Son Ltd of Shelton, who had managed to produce such a magnificent cake during such times of shortage. Father Ryan, by now an old friend of the family, sat at the top of the table together with Father O'Connor. The wedding was reported as follows in the Evening Sentinel of 11th September 1948.

WEDDINGS IN NORTH STAFFORDSHIRE: Well-known families united in Goldenhill Ceremony. Nuptial Mass was celebrated on September the 9th at St Joseph's Roman Catholic Church, Goldenhill, for the marriage of Mr Ettore Emanuelli, son of Mr and Mrs Giovanni Emanuelli of 273 High Street. Tunstall, and Miss Margaret Joan Hulse S. R. N. only daughter of Mr and Mrs R. T. Hulse of 18 Church Street Goldenhill. The couple, who are spending their honeymoon in Florence and Rome, are to be received in audience by the Pope. The bride was attired in a classical gown of white georgette with high neckline and bishop's sleeves. She wore a headdress of orange blossom and carried an ivory-bound prayer book and a bouquet of arum lilies and white carnations. Four bridesmaids were in attendance. Miss Mary Waring, cousin of the bride, and Miss Annunciata Tedaldi, cousin of the bridegroom. They wore Tudor-style gowns of hyacinth blue crêpe-de-chine and carried bouquets of *scabious and pink roses*, and Miss Sandra Critchley cousin of the bride and Miss Anne Walkley, who wore dresses of embossed primrose nylon trimmed with tangerine ribbon, and carried baskets of pink roses. Mr Louis Emanuelli, brother of the bridegroom, was the best man, and the groomsmen were Mr Aldo Emanuelli and Mr. R. L. Hulse, Mr. Tom Wheetman and Mr S. Chadwick. The Reverend Father T. O'Connor, parish priest, officiated at the ceremony, at which Schubert's Ave Maria was sung by Mr. Michael Gilligan. The organist was Mr. J. Miller. The reception was held at the George Hotel Burslem, where 100 guests were entertained.*

After the reception and a quick change of clothing we were whisked away to Crewe Station for the train to London Euston. Much to our embarrassment, we were showered with confetti as we boarded the train. As we waved goodbye, Joan's mother called out to her. 'Joan, don't forget to write to us as soon as you get to Rome!' Joan promised she would. Here is her letter:

Imperial Hotel
Rome
14-9-48

Dear Mum, Dad and Reg,
How are you all at home? I suppose you have been busy tying up all the loose strings after the wedding. Hector and I are very well up to the present moment, so don't worry about either of us.

We had a good trip down to London, but we did feel silly sitting amongst all that confetti. Two men who got on the same train and sat in opposite seats said 'I hope they don't think it's us!'

The hotel where we stayed the night was scrupulously clean, but before we turned in we had a walk round and saw Hyde Park from the outside. As it was pretty dark by then we also saw Buckingham Palace with the sentries standing outside the gates. As we were about to pass one of the small cafes, Hector noticed an Italian whom he knew during his internment so of course he went in and chatted for a while.

On the way down from London to Dover the following morning our seats were faced by a doctor and his wife on the train. Just before the train pulled out a young man appeared very breathlessly on the platform to wave them goodbye. 'Oh! The darling,' she said. 'That's my son you know.' Then she began to tell us about her married daughter and the son who had just turned up so unexpectedly at the last moment. Because Hector and I are fairly good listeners she seemed to take a fancy to us so that when we got off the train to take the boat they were still following behind. When the customs man looked in my handbag she said 'So this is what you get on your honeymoon!' He didn't bother any further then.

We had just landed on the boat and were looking around to see what was what, when we came upon the doctor and his wife again. Mrs Austin waved her arm wildly at us, so we went over to her. 'I've bagged you two seats,' she said.' 'I hope you don't mind, but later when the rush has settled down there will be an awful scramble for seats.'

Later on they took us down to the bar to have a drink. Hector had a peculiar drink with mineral water, quinine and gin mixed together. I had a shandy. The sea was very smooth and I so happened to see the white cliffs of Dover to their best advantage. Finally, when we landed in Calais there was a rush to get off the boat and for the trains. We then lost sight of Mr and Mrs Austin (the doctor and his wife) and to tell you the truth I was a bit sorry because they had been so companionable.

On the Rome Express our companions were as silent as the doctor's wife was voluble, but we didn't mind as we were too busy looking at the scenery. I was a bit disappointed in France; it was very much like the fields of Cheshire, flat with small hedges separating one field from another. The houses, which were built of stone, had a parched look and the woodwork needed a coat of paint badly, even the fields look parched. We had our lunch on the train. It consisted of five courses at the end of which I felt almost too fat to rise from my seat.

Our first stop was at Paris, where we had to get out to have dinner at the hotel Terminus which was opposite the station, this meal consisted of three courses, one of which was beefsteak and chips. After that Hector and I waddled back to the station as fast as we could get to relieve our fellow passengers, who had agreed to take it in turns with us watching our luggage. We were glad to get back to the station as it was raining by then. An hour later we began our journey again and this was to prove the most fatiguing part of all. We travelled all through the night, dozing off as we sat there, so you can imagine how tired we felt. Strangely enough this tiredness passed away the following morning, especially when we saw the mountains of Switzerland. They were indescribably beautiful. In the hollows and the valleys, wreaths of mist curled around like a fine white veil of chiffon.

The train passed on by Lake Maggiore, which is very vast in size. Far behind us in the background could still be observed the snow peaked mountains of Switzerland. All the houses there looked very pretty with their red roofs and yellow or cream walls, they have many verandas with hanging pots of flowers, between the houses are interspaced tall trees, shrubbery and gardens, which make the cream and the red colours of the houses contrast very effectively. Every inch of ground is cultivated even down to the lip of Lake Maggiore. Pines cover the sides of the hills, which often drop down into deep ravines.

The scenery was very much the same going further into Italy, flattening out as we reached the cities into small hills and plains. At last we landed in Rome, tired and weary and feeling a little sick also with the good food and continuous motion.

We struggled from our train with our luggage to the station entrance and managed to get a taxi. Before we left the station a Roman woman who had been in the same compartment gave us her telephone number so that we could ring her up whilst we were in Rome in case we got lonely.

We arrived at the Hotel Imperial at 1 a.m. on Sunday morning feeling as though we could drop down in our tracks. I must close now, but I shall write again soon.

Your loving daughter

Joan xxx

Tying the Knot 129

Louis and Father Ryan at the reception in Burslem. Father Ryan had championed my cause during my internment.

My mother and father on their son's big day! Cheers!

The happy couple, September 1948. The beauty of my English Rose took my breath away when she walked down the aisle!

The wedding party, from left to right: Annunciata Tedaldi, my parents, Louis, myself, Joan, Joan's parents, Mary Waring, the little girls, Anne Walkley and Sandra Critchley.

What a cake!

CHAPTER 12

Luna di Miele

'*Ella si va, sentendosi laudare,
benignamente d'umiltà vestuta;
e par che sia una cosa venuta
da cielo in terra a miracol mostrare.*'*
Dante Alighieri, La Vita Nuova, Capitolo XXVI

The night air was still warm and balmy as we arrived at the Hotel Imperiale. At last we were in Rome and our honeymoon could begin in earnest! I hoped that this visit would erase the painful memories of my last stay in Rome at the *Campo Mussolini* back in 1939.

We checked in. A bevy of liveried porters fussed over our bags and whisked them away. Both Joan and I were staggered by the opulence as we were shown into our honeymoon suite. It was like walking onto a Hollywood film set. Marble everywhere! Crystal chandeliers, flowers in every corner, and the magnificent '*letto matrimoniale.*' We threw open the windows and drank a glass of champagne, toasting the moon in the deep ultramarine sky. The Via Veneto, which passed beneath our windows, was still lively even at that late hour. Joan was enchanted.

---

* She passes, hearing herself praised, clad in
kindly humility, and seems to have come upon earth
from heaven to make show of a miracle.

The following morning, before venturing out into the warm morning air of our first day in Rome, we breakfasted in the magnificent dining room. As a caterer, I greatly appreciated the creamy cappuccino, still almost unknown in England at that time, and briefly weighed up the chances of launching it successfully in the Potteries, and quickly dismissed them! And then there were the delicious brioches, croissants and pastries. After breakfast, we admired the stylish cafes and bars along the famed Via Veneto, the street that was to become synonymous with the 'dolce vita' made famous by Federico Fellini, Marcello Mastroianni and Anita Ekberg. Joan and I already felt like film stars! I was so proud of her. She was magnificently elegant. The Italian men turned to watch her pass as she went by. She was my Beatrice and my Laura all in one!

There was one place that Joan was very keen to visit: the catacombs! Personally, I wouldn't be seen dead in the catacombs, but I was pleased to accompany Joan, and we spent a little time in the eerie depths before emerging into the Roman sun. I suggested we take a stroll along the Appian Way. 'Ooh! The Via Appia? Couldn't be 'appier!' joked Joan. She was in a good mood after her visit to the catacombs and she was looking forward to visiting the ossuary in the church opposite the hotel before dinner!

For my part, I was burning to see the Galleria Borghese. The gallery is housed in the Villa Borghese, which in turn is set in the Villa Borghese gardens, a large heart-shaped park just north of the centre of Rome, one of the city's grandest public parks, boasting plane trees, yews, oleanders, cypresses, magnolias and other exotic plants interspersed with busts of illustrious Italians, and groups of statuary. We saw Canova's carving of Paulina Borghese, depicted as Venus Victrix reclining on a couch in a most sensual pose. Paulina was Napoleon's sister and it was at his instigation that she married Prince Borghese. We also admired Raphael's beautiful and mysterious painting, the Baker's Daughter, or *La Fornarina* as it is called in Italian.

After a day of sightseeing and art galleries we returned to the hotel where the *concierge* pulled me to one side and explained that he was aware that we were to have an audience with the Pope. The official invitation, he said, would come from the Vatican and we were not to be disappointed if this took a few days to come through. He assured me that as soon as it arrived he would let me know. I thanked him. This was indeed going to be a most fantastic Roman Holiday.

During the next few days we saw the Trevi Fountain, the Spanish Steps, Piazza Navona, the Foro Romano, the Sistine Chapel. Finally, one evening on our return to the Imperiale the concierge came to us smiling and said '*Ecco, è arrivato l'invito* – your invitation has come!'

There it was at last. The audience was scheduled for the afternoon of the following day. The Pope, it appears, was in residence at his summer retreat at Castel Gandolfo outside Rome in the Alban hills. Protocol decreed that ladies were to wear long gloves and an appropriate head covering. Immediately after dinner Joan and I went shopping in the busy Via Veneto, where Joan purchased a pair of long-sleeved black lace gloves and a matching black lace mantilla.

The next morning, after a late and leisurely breakfast we retired to our room to prepare ourselves for the momentous occasion. We were both nervous. Joan kept checking her dress, trying on her long gloves and headscarf. Dutch courage came with a glass or two of *prosecco*. A tap at our door, a final check and we made our way down the corridor through the spacious lounge and onto the Via Veneto. Our car was waiting to take us to Castel Gandolfo. Our driver headed south and out of the city limits. In no time at all we were in open countryside as we approached the Alban Hills. We passed through the vineyards noted for the Frascati wine which we enjoyed with our evening dinners.

On our arrival, we were ushered into a beautifully furnished salon. Wall paintings, velvet drapes and chandeliers gave the room a sense of tranquillity and yet timelessness. A faint scent of incense struck us. There were several other couples waiting. This was not to be a purely private audience, for which we were extremely grateful! Some fifteen minutes passed and then without announcement Pope Pious XII strolled into the room through a side door. He was accompanied by a cardinal.

Pious was a slender figure with a benign expression, bespectacled and wearing a long ivory coloured robe with a shoulder cape and a small skull cap. He welcomed us in perfect English and Italian, and gave a short homily on the sanctity of marriage. He then approached us very informally, giving us his papal blessing. In turn, we inclined our heads, making the sign of the cross. It was all over within a matter of minutes, a truly moving and spiritual experience. Moist-eyed we were ushered into an antechamber where we were given a commemorative medal of the occasion.

In what appeared to be no time at all we were back at the Hotel Imperiale. At dinner that evening we celebrated with an extra glass of Frascati wine.

On our last day in Rome we climbed to the roof of St. Peter's Basilica to enjoy the view of the city. It proved to be quite a way to the top, but as we stood alongside the statues of the Apostles we were rewarded by a moving panorama. Looking down on to the square enclosed by the embracing arms of Bernini's colonnade and down the Via della Conciliazione, with the whole city before us, I put my arm around Joan's waist and whispered in her ear 'Arriverderci Roma!'

The next day we boarded the train for Florence. The *Children's Encyclopaedia* that my father had so kindly bought me as a child had instilled in me a love and interest in the Florentine renaissance. As I grew older, especially during my internment, I had read Vasari's 'Lives of the Painters.' Some of my fellow internees had been learned men and had given lectures on Florence and its literature, arts, architecture and politics, so I felt very much 'at home' when we arrived in Florence for the second part of our honeymoon. The names were those of old friends: the Medici palaces, Brunelleschi's

Dome, Giotto's Tower, the churches of Santa Croce, Santa Maria Novella, the Uffizi, the Pitti Palace, the Ponte Vecchio. My childhood dreams were finally coming true.

Thomas Cook had booked us into the Hotel Bonciani, which was housed in the Palazzo Pitti Broccardi on the Via dei Panzani between Piazza Santa Maria Novella and Piazza dell'Unità d'Italia. The agency had chosen well. The Bonciani was a typical Florentine palazzo, well carpeted and not wanting in any of the luxuries we had become to expect. Escorting us to our room the manager threw open the door and extending his arm with a flourish announced '*Ecco la sala di Garibaldi*!' General Giuseppe Garibaldi had stayed there in 1840, he explained. Over the bed hung a large portrait of the red-shirted patriot. It was indeed a privilege to be accommodated in such a room, and Joan found Garibaldi rather striking, which made *me* rather jealous!

During the next few days, we visited many art galleries and churches: the Uffizi, the Pitti, the Palazzo Vecchio, the Galleria dell'Accademia, the Duomo. I still recall to this day the thrill of standing before Botticelli's Birth of Venus in the Uffizi. Joan was greatly impressed by the beautiful Basilica di Santa Croce: its cloister boasts a tablet dedicated to Florence Nightingale, who was born in Florence. The basilica is famed as Italy's Westminster Abbey. Michelangelo, Alberti, Machiavelli, Galileo Galilei, and Rossini are all buried there.

But mental indigestion was now beginning to set in, and so we decided to take a break and have a day in the countryside and visit the hill-top town of Fiesole.

We left the Bonciani early in the morning after breakfast. The lovely hill-top town of Fiesole dates to Etruscan times. There are still traces of its fortified walls. It boasts a fine Roman amphitheatre. The town nestles among hills, looking down on the city of Florence and the river Arno on its way down to Pisa. We spent some time wandering through the narrow streets and squares and took a leisurely lunch at a trattoria in Piazza Mino. After lunch, we sat on the cool steps of the Roman amphitheatre and took in the views of the surrounding hills. It was so peaceful after the bustle of Florence's busy streets. We strolled hand in hand admiring the view. The sun was beginning to set. This was without doubt the finest viewpoint of the city of Florence, the sun catching the red roofs, the Duomo with Giotto's campanile. As we admired the view, faint strains of accordion music accompanied by sounds of laughter drifted up to us from the village below.

The evening breeze was rustling the silver-green leaves of the olive trees as we took our last glimpse of Florence below. Alas it was time to end what had been a restoring and romantic day in Fiesole. Back to the Bonciani to pack our bags. On the following day we were to leave for Parma, and then on to Genoa.

When I first planned our honeymoon it was never my intention to include Genoa in the list of places to be visited. It was as we boarded the train at Crewe that my mother approached me and said 'Now you not forget to take Joan to visit the Sanctuary of La Madonna della Guardia?'. 'Yes,' I said. 'I promise that we shall do so!' I had often heard my mother mention the sanctuary at home, but did not at the time take much notice. I imagine that as a young girl she would have made pilgrimages there together with friends or relatives. It was not very far from Bardi.

The sanctuary, it transpired, was at the summit of Monte Figogna at some 800 meters above sea level in the Ligurian hills roughly twenty kilometres from Genoa. Monte Figogna, sometimes called Monte La Guardia, had been – as the name implies – the seat many years before of a watchtower that looked out over the Ligurian sea providing a look-out for any hostile forces which might imperil the Genovese Republic.

The sanctuary's story dates back to the year 1490. It was on the 29 August of that year that Our Lady appeared to a local shepherd by the name of Benedetto Pareto. During the centuries that followed the apparition the number of pilgrims increased, with each succeeding generation enlarging and embellishing the shrine. Today a magnificent sanctuary exists with hospices for travellers, its interior decorated with discarded crutches and the like, left there as testimony of the many cures attributed to the Madonna della Guardia.

Joan and I were impressed and understood why my mother was so keen that we visit the Sanctuary. I was glad that I had kept my promise and taken Joan to see what must have been a very special place for my religious and pious mother.

But now Bardi was beckoning and it was time to leave Genoa. We returned to the Belle Vue Hotel where we had been staying to make our travel arrangements.

Hidden away in the northern Apennines, Bardi has never been an easy place to get to. There is no rail link and in 1948 the roads were hazardous and liable to landslides. I remember how they kept climbing higher and higher through the woods with hair-raising bends that never seemed to come to an end.

At last with a cry of delight I caught sight in the distance of the Castello di Bardi. It still stood brooding over the confluence of the Ceno and the Noveglia, clothed in autumnal mist which dissolved as we drew near, revealing the castle perched on its red-veined jasper rock. It was pure magic. Joan was enchanted. 'The perfect setting for a gothic novel,' she said. 'Has it got dungeons?'

In 1927 my uncle Antonio Tedaldi and my maternal grandfather Giovanni Tedaldi were farming at Barzia di Sotto. In 1939 they had moved to Cogno di Grezzo, which was where I had taken refuge with them after my summer camp fiascos in Rome and Pescara. Always trying to improve their lot, they had moved again and were now at Corti di Sopra, a small hamlet just outside but still within walking distance of Bardi. Grandfather was no longer alive, but uncle Toni and his sons Pierino, Angelo and Bertino ran the farm together with his wife Maria. They were overjoyed to see us and we were immediately made to feel at home and part of the family.

Any my fears I might have had that Joan would dislike the primitive conditions and the simple way of life were completely unfounded. My English rose blossomed in the autumnal Italian sun. She was radiant in this bucolic Bardi and did not miss the comforts of the fine hotels we had got to know in Florence and Rome. My Italian family fell in love with Joan at a stroke. She was so modest and shy and so happy to be in the countryside that they could not fail but love her. Joan fell head over heels in love with the oxen that my uncle used on the farm, she would stroke and fondle them and in turn they would nudge her lovingly whenever she passed by. They were working beasts and were not used to being caressed in this way and seemed to enjoy it immensely. Magically, they were called Moro and Toro, just as when I had been there more than ten years before.

Joan and I took frequent walks in the nearby vineyards and among the chestnut trees. We would walk down into Bardi to sit and chat in the Piccolo Bar with the other *'inglesi'* who were also visiting their relatives. This was a pleasure for Joan as she was able to speak to them in English, while at the farm I had to translate for her. They spoke in gentle Welsh accents, often of the war, which was still such a painful memory!

We visited my mother's relatives and friends. Although they were complete strangers to me, I was pleased to meet them. They were part of my Italian roots. They lived in hamlets and smallholdings among the neighbouring hills and so we visited them accompanied by my cousin Angelo. I walked the mountain tracks, with Joan beside me on horseback. We had a wonderful time. We were feasted and given too much to drink.

Alas our time in Bardi was coming to its close, soon it would be time to return home to Tunstall and the family business. Time to say goodbye to Bardi. When, I wondered, should I ever return to this magic place?

I have often asked myself what compels so many second- and third-generation emigrants from Bardi to return every August to celebrate the *'Festa degli Emigranti.'* They come from all over the world, South Wales, England, Scotland, the Americas, New Zealand, and on such days you can walk the streets of Bardi and hear hardly a word of Italian spoken. All the same, they are still all Bardigiani at heart!

And so with tears and fond embraces we said farewell and made our way to Parma and the train journey back to the Channel. It was a simply terrible crossing. The boat was tossed about like a cork. We both suffered awfully from seasickness and we were quite ill when we reached England. We booked into the Regent Palace Hotel in London, where we asked the hotel receptionist to book us into a theatre show in order to cheer ourselves up a little. They got us tickets for the Victoria Palace where we saw the Crazy Gang. If I am not mistaken, the show was called 'Together Again.'

Our honeymoon was over and now it was time to get back to work!

Joan in Ostia on the coast near Rome, 1948. 'Much nicer than Blackpool,' she said!

Joan enjoying the sun in Villa Borghese.

Luna di Miele 143

Our honeymoon hotel on the Via Veneto.

My English Rose in Nervi on the Ligurian coast near Genoa.

Joan ringing the bells in Pisa, 1948.

Joan admiring the view from Fiesole.

Le campagnole! Zia Maria and Joan in Bardi.

Joan loved the oxen in Bardi. On the right Zio Toni.

CHAPTER 13

A Booming Business

> *'Chi vuol esser lieto, sia:*
> *di doman non c'è certezza'**
> Lorenzo dei Medici, Canzone di Bacco

My brother Louis and I were now married men. It was not long before our first children arrived. Joan gave birth to our daughter Marguerite Antionette in early 1949 and Dorina to her son Paul Sebastiano later in the same year. Now not only married men, but fathers, too, we set about locating a site for our new project with due earnestness and increased vigour: we were looking for a site for an ultra-modern ice-cream factory.

We soon found what we were looking for. The property was known as 'The Paddock.' This consisted of three and a half acres of land on the outskirts of the small town of Biddulph, not far from Tunstall. It boasted a four-bedroom residence, with landscaped gardens and lawns, a tennis court, a boating pool, greenhouses, orchards, a summer house. There were also some single-storey buildings which we earmarked to become our 'Factory in a Garden' as we were to baptise it. Once again, as with the Cafe Continental, we were faced with

---

* Let him be merry who will be:
there is no certainty for tomorrow.

endless red tape and meetings with sanitary and food inspectors. We needed to find and purchase the latest manufacturing equipment: stainless steel pasteurising vats, ageing vats, surface coolers, homogenisers, continuous freezers, a chocolate enrobing machine for the production of choc ices, a briquette-wrapping machine, cold stores. Louis and I went down to London to find it.

Every year in October the National Dairy Show was held at Olympia in London. At that time this was the capital's main exhibition centre. In addition to the milk and dairy industry, a good part of the exhibition was devoted to the expanding and growing ice-cream trade. Louis and I combed the hundreds of exhibition stands devoted to the very latest developments in ice-cream making. Firms such as T. Giusti and son of London would exhibit the very latest in stainless steel equipment, freezers and pasteurising vats. Every aspect of the trade was catered for. Ice-cream tricycles from W. R. Pashley and Mattiello of Birmingham. Coach-builders specialised in ice-cream vans, wafer biscuit manufacturers such as Valvona of Manchester and Facchino's of Birmingham were all represented. This was the highlight of the year for ice-cream makers and caterers throughout the country, and an opportunity for them to view the latest advances in manufacturing techniques and to place their orders for new equipment.

We found virtually everything we needed at the National Dairy Show. It was delivered and installed in the course of 1949 and after a year of hard work the factory was officially opened in March 1950 in the presence of the Medical Officer of Health Dr. J. Ferguson and other dignitaries from Biddulph Urban District Council. The trade magazine Ice Cream Topics reported as follows:

Emanuelli's Factory in a Garden

We have at last seen an ice-cream factory actually situated in a garden, with a competent gardener in attendance (his house

A Booming Business

is on the other side of the lawn), flowers growing under glass as well as in the open, a tennis court, a swimming pool, and many other amenities. The 3½-acre estate is known as The Paddock, Biddulph. It entailed a journey from London, but we are more than pleased that we visited the factory when it was officially opened on Thursday, March 23rd. And our first reaction to the gleaming white rooms, spotless machinery and staff, and well-deserved compliments paid to G. Emanuelli and his family by several speakers and many visitors is that the trade is best left in the hands of old-established traders: they alone develop the badly-needed touch or feel.

G. Emanuelli picked up the trade in S. Wales quite a number of years ago. But he picked it with care, always tried to improve and invariably did improve. By the time he opened up in Tunstall, Staffs, he was unchallengeable as an ice-cream manufacturer and refreshment caterer. In fact, when his Cafe Continental, so elegant and even, in some respects, novel, was opened in the High Street two years ago, there were some who stated that it was no more than could be expected from experienced father and enterprising sons.

But this new factory could not have been expected. It is definitely a big stride forward and should suffice the firm for many years to come. The layout is perfect, thanks to plenty of doors, delivery accommodation, etc. Goods from the receiving and storage rooms find their way to the necessary processing: from then onwards. Creamery package equipment mainly sees to all the necessary heating, pasteurising, homogenising, cooling, ageing, freezing, hardening and storage, cutting, dipping and wrapping. A fleet of really attractively painted vans, which carry coloured reproductions of the famous Bardi windows in stained glass and which visitors to the firm's cafe never fail to admire, sees to deliveries, for wholesale and retail, throughout the Potteries. In this district ice cream is preferred white or creamy white, but it must also be rich, smooth and sweet. Emanuelli & Sons know this, keep to it and maintain it in the superlative. Ice Cream Topics, Achille Pompa, April 1950.

Sales shot through the roof in the first year of operation. We were proving to be a good team. Louis managed production while I looked after marketing and Aldo ran the cafes.

Shortly after the factory was opened, Joan gave birth to our son Anthony John. Now, with a growing family, a large house, an increasingly busy social life and a demanding business, we were in need of domestic help. My mother was acquainted with a family back home in Bardi. They had two daughters, Gina and Delfina Assirati, who – like so many generations of Bardigiani before them – were keen to find jobs abroad. The necessary permits were obtained from the local authorities and they came to work for us. Gina came to The Paddock at Biddulph as an au pair and nanny for the children. Delfina worked as a waitress at the Cafe Continental at Tunstall.

Delfina was the younger of the two sisters. Before leaving Italy she had been an extra in the Giuseppe de Santis neo-realist film '*Riso Amaro* – Bitter Rice' starring Silvana Mangano, Vittorio Gassman and Doris Dowling. This much-acclaimed film was set in the rice fields of the Po valley in northern Italy. The film was an honest attempt to portray social inequity in a post-war Italy that remained scarred by the recent global conflict. But it hit the headlines and found favour with the public for quite other reasons: scantily-clad young women toiling in the rice fields of the Po valley drew crowds that Rossellini with his austere *'Roma, Città Aperta'* and De Sica with his *'Ladri di Bicicletta'* could only have dreamt off!

The film was shown at the Ritz Cinema, directly opposite the Cafe Continental. The manager of the Ritz, being acquainted with my father, found out that Delfina had played in the film. Shrewd as he was, he invited Delfina to come to the cinema and say a few words of introduction before the film. With her dark good looks she attracted a lot of attention that evening. The film drew large audiences in Tunstall. Our cafe Continental seemed to benefit, too. We noticed a distinct increase in the number of young male customers for several months after the film had been shown.

While the new ice-cream factory thrived, the Cafe Continental was awarded some prestigious orders. In February 1951 we were asked to cater for the funeral of Father P. J. Ryan. This was a great honour and a momentous occasion. Father Ryan had lived in Tunstall since 1899 and he was an immensely prominent local personality and much-loved by the Catholic community. His funeral service filled the Sacred Heart Church and the procession that wound its way through the streets of the town to Clay Hills cemetery drew huge crowds paying their last tribute to this great Irishman.

After the funeral, dozens of Father Ryan's former seminary and college friends and other priests and clergy gathered in the crypt of the Church of the Sacred Heart in Tunstall to pay their last respects. They were obviously all very pleased to see each other again. Despite the sad circumstances and eerie venue, a very jolly 'party' of Chaucerian dimensions was soon in full swing. As caterers, we were responsible for the food and drink, and lashings of both were consumed. I've never since seen so many priests having such a good time! I should be loathe to use the word 'orgy,' but earthly pleasures were certainly not eschewed. I am in no doubt that Father Ryan would have approved.

Back at the ice-cream factory, one of my earliest marketing exercises was to organise a garden party, which we held in 1951 in the grounds of 'The Paddock' to celebrate the Festival of Britain. We invited retailers who sold Emanuel's ices. Special gateaux were produced featuring the Festival logo. This marketing measure had a notable and positive impact on sales.

As marketing manager I was also involved in the activities of the North Staffs branch of the so-called 'Ice Cream Alliance.' This was a national organisation devoted to promoting the interests of the growing numbers of ice-cream manufacturers throughout the country. It addressed matters of legislation and official restrictions imposed on the industry. I was vice-chairman of the North Staffs branch. My good friend John Ashmore of Ashmore's Ice Cream of Uttoxeter was the chairman.

These were golden times for the firm of Emanuel & Sons. Everything was running like clockwork. The family was becoming affluent. My brothers and I worked very hard, sometimes not getting to bed before the early hours. Besides the cafes in Tunstall and the 'Factory in a Garden,' we were now also running a small but growing fleet of ice-cream vans out of Biddulph. We pursued a three-pronged business plan. First, we ran our own cafes, which we supplied with ice-cream from the new factory and which generated a steady cash flow. Second, we supplied retailers and the entertainment industry throughout Staffordshire with our ice cream, and third our growing fleet of ice-cream vans was rapidly conquering the suburbs of Stoke-on-Trent.

The van business was developing very well. In the mornings we would send the vans out into the surrounding council estates, which were growing fast in those days. In the evenings the van salesmen would return from their rounds to hand over their takings and tell tales of 'unfair' competition. This might simply be rival ice-cream vendors leapfrogging them on their rounds, but it could easily escalate into fisticuffs and acts of 'sabotage.' I remember stories of nails being thrown into the path of our vans. A veritable ice-cream war!

Such matters would be raised at the monthly meetings of the North Staffs branch of the trade-association, 'The Ice Cream Alliance.' Verbal agreements would be made, only to be broken whenever an overzealous salesman encroached on a competitor's allotted round.

There was no Catholic church in Biddulph in the early fifties and in order to raise funds for the building of a new church, we organised garden parties and fêtes at 'The Paddock.' On one such occasion, as a member of the Knights of Saint Columba I had the great honour to be able to invite the Right Reverend Bishop Humphrey Bright with his attendant clergy to just such a garden party. Many local dignitaries also attended, including the Chairman of the Biddulph District Council and the Clerk of the Council. I recall it was a beautiful day. The grounds of 'The Paddock' were festooned with colourful bunting. The event was a great success. A few years later a new church was finally built for the Catholic community in Biddulph, the 'Church of the English Martyrs' and from then on the Knights of Saint Columba met in its loft.

Back in Tunstall, the Cafe Continental was also enjoying growing local prestige. The North Stafford Hotel called me one day to ask if we could look after the celebrated Italian tenor Luigi Infantino, who was appearing in concert at the Victoria Hall in Hanley. I agreed immediately. I picked him up in the Hillman Minx and drove him over to Tunstall. He explained he got very lonely staying at hotels and that he liked to spend time with compatriots whenever possible. The Cafe Continental was the first establishment that had occurred to the manager of the hotel. Meanwhile, with Delfina's help my mother had set the table with her best white linen tablecloth, her Royal Doulton tableware. Heads turned as I escorted Luigi Infantino through the cafe, his dark good looks and elegant suit were striking. Introductions all around. Much handshaking and polite Italian phrases – '*Molto gentile, grazie! Il piacere è tutto mio!*' The scene was one of unmitigated cordiality. Mother had prepared a wonderful minestrone, followed by a steaming dish of ravioli 'peasant style' with abundant servings of parmesan cheese. Father was lavish with his favourite wines. The atmosphere was very jolly. Before I took Signor Infantino back to the hotel he gave us all signed photographs and tickets for the performance. With a great flourish he also signed my mother's best tablecloth. I'm not sure she appreciated that! That evening he sang like an angel. His rendering of 'Santa Lucia' was world-class. Was it mother's ravioli, I wondered, that had put him in such good voice?

So business and the social side of life were both booming. My involvement with the Ice Cream Alliance and the Knights of Columba meant that both Joan and I were able to indulge in a little light relief from business. We attended the dinner dances held by the two organisations. Following the austerities and limitations of the war years, these events were a welcome diversion and the ladies in particular took every occasion to indulge in the very latest fashion in eye-catching gowns and jewellery and the men were always in tails or dinner jackets. Guests and representatives of the trade would attend from throughout the Midlands and often we would be graced with the presence of the national president. Whenever possible we would get a celebrity to attend the Alliance dinners and I well recall – to the delight of our ladies – a visit by the handsome Dickie Valentine, a singer who was very popular with the ladies in the fifties.

The Knights of Saint Columba dinners were occasions of great elegance that I look back on with nostalgia. We also attended occasions such as the Saint Patrick's Night Ball and the Annual Cinema Ball. These events were held at the King's Hall at Stoke. The Hall was always beautifully decked out with flowers and there, too, we would invite celebrities. I especially recall Deborah Kerr and Chips Rafferty.

In 1954 our second daughter, Alda Maria Silvia, was born. We named her Alda after my brother Aldo, Maria because she was born in the Marian year, and Silvia after the saint's name on whose day she happened to have been born. Four years later our second son, Domenic Peter, arrived. The house was full of children. Business was booming, I was a member of various societies and clubs, the children were going to good schools and taking riding and dancing lessons. Our house was spacious and surrounded by elegant gardens. I was at the peak of my powers. The deprivations and humiliations of the 1930s and the war seemed a long way behind us. I had arrived! Or at least that is what I thought.

The factory opening in March 1950. Achille Pompa between myself and my father.

The new ice-cream factory and our ice-cream vans in 1951. We raised the Union Flag to celebrate the Festival of Britain.

156 A SENSE OF BELONGING

Bishop Bright and other dignitaries in the gardens of The Paddock at a fund-raising effort for a new Catholic Church in Biddulph, 1950.

'Emanuel & Son's First Annual At-Home took place in brilliant sunshine on Thursday, August 2nd 1951 in the gardens of their model ice-cream factory, known as The Paddock Biddulph, which is probably unique in our trade for beauty of situation, attractive layout and combination of amenities.' Ice Cream Topics, 1951.

Biddulph 1950. Back row: Louis, Pierino Tedaldi, Delfina Assirati, my father, Joan's father and brother, Aldo. Front row: my mother with Louis' son Paul, Dorina, Joan with Anthony, Marguerite, Joan's mother, myself.

Our new home 'The Paddock' with tennis court and boating lake and a beautiful view of the countryside.

Artist and friend Jack Simcock painted this portrait of me in the early 1950s.

Joan and I danced the nights away . . .

. . . all through the fifties!

CHAPTER 14

The Great Meltdown

What goes up must come down!

The sixties mean different things to many people. It all depends, I suppose, on how old you were at the time. Looking back over almost half a century. I recall the Post Office Tower in London ushering in the age of modern technology, and the Sydney Harbour Opera House bringing new ideas into modern architecture. I associate the sixties with what became to be known as 'The Swinging Sixties.' Carnaby Street and the first see-through dress, split skirts and revealing blouses, Mick Jagger and the Rolling Stones, the Beatles, Martin Luther King, the Vietnam War, the death of President Kennedy and Winston Churchill. Student revolts at the Sorbonne in Paris and in London. The E-type Jaguar. The fountain pen made way for the ball-point pen, which eventually would make way for the computer. The QE II was launched from John Brown's shipyard and was to become Britain's premier cross-channel and cruise liner.

This was the age of the hippies, mods and rockers, free love and flower power. Youth was taking over. Peace would replace war. Where did it all go wrong I often wonder. Pop festivals at the Isle of Wight and at Woodstock. Drugs were freely available at these events: three days of youthful excesses and the crowds were so large that it was impossible to hear the music and the more outrageous the clothing one wore, the more acceptable you were to your fellows.

You will have gathered by now, I am sure, that the sixties do not hold a special place in my heart. But one of the few events that I remember with great pleasure was the birth of our last child: Michael Paul was born on the 11 November 1963. Our family was now complete.

Overall, however, I look back with great sadness on the sixties. It was during this period that my wife Joan fell into a depression which lasted many years. She became increasingly withdrawn, introspective, apathetic and irascible. This put great strains on family life. Although I sought medical advice, no help was forthcoming and Joan's depression became ever deeper.

At the same time, the sixties saw the tide begin to turn against the business fortunes of the Emanuelli family. With the relaxation of the restrictions with regard to rationing and other matters, the 'Big Boys' came onto the scene. Lyons Maid (J. Lyons & Co. Ltd.) and Walls Ice Cream (Lever Bros) were beginning to dominate the ice-cream trade, gradually wresting trade away from small and medium-sized family companies. With extensive national advertising and eye-catching point-of-sale material they began to take over the business of smaller manufacturers – such as ourselves. Exorbitant discounts were offered to retailers and refrigerators were installed free on their premises, meaning we were unable to compete. Every corner shop now sold the nationally advertised brands, you could get your ice cream from garage forecourts, the off-licence and even school tuck shops, and even butchers and greengrocers were competing for their share of the trade. Finally, increasing competition also came from the supermarkets, which were now selling all the well-known brands: Lyons Maid, Walls and other national brands were all to be found in their display cabinets.

Likewise, the cinema trade was fitted out with refrigerators free of charge, and uniforms and illuminated trays were provided for the sales girls. The inevitable outcome of all this

The Great Meltdown

was that we lost our cinema contracts and also many of our retail customers.

Having invested in the very latest state-of-the-art equipment we now found that production at our factory was almost at a standstill. What's more, our business had melted down almost entirely to street trading and Walls and Lyons also entered this segment of the market, flooding the streets with their vans. This, together with their national advertising campaigns, made the van trade even more competitive.

Competent salesmen were becoming exceedingly difficult to recruit, when we did succeed we were constrained to pay them over the winter months in order to be sure of their services when the 'season' started again in the spring. We employed them to do maintenance, gardening and landscaping work in the gardens of 'The Paddock.' This was not always successful. In many cases, at the start of the new season they would purchase their own vans and would then be yet another competitive seller on the streets.

The excessive numbers of vans on the roads was becoming a public nuisance and complaints from the public over the use of the chimes which heralded one van after another on the streets of the housing estates resulted in many fines. Competition became even more intense and ice-cream street wars became the order of the day.

As a small family business we were heavily reliant on the banks and my brothers and I kept pumping our own savings in order to keep the firm trading.

Finally, hoping to benefit from the latest fashion in ice-cream street trading, namely soft ice cream, we decided to enter into a franchise agreement with J. Lyons and Co, Ltd. in which we were to operate a fleet of Mister Softee ice-cream vehicles. These vans came complete with their own on-board generators which operated the on-board soft-serve freezers.

The terms of the franchise agreement stipulated that we buy the ice-cream mix from J. Lyons and Co. Ltd. This rendered our 'Factory in a Garden' obsolete. We also had to conform to the cone-sizes and prices as laid down by their national advertising policy. We took a half-page advertisement in the Evening Sentinel at some considerable expense to the effect that 'Emanuel & Sons would supply Mister Softee ice cream throughout the streets of the Potteries. It was bitter to say good-bye to the long tradition of ice-cream making my father had built up. The inane Mister Softee jingle we were obliged to use for the vans still haunts me:

> *'Listen for my store on wheels, ding-a-ling down the street.*
> *The creamiest, dreamiest soft ice cream,*
> *You get from Mister Softee.'*

But for a while at least the decision to stop manufacturing our own products proved to be the right one. Then, however, new competition in the form of Mr. Whippy came onto the scene. This firm operated similar vehicles with on-board soft-serve freezers. This was followed by other independent one-man outfits who had spotted their chance, bought their own vans and fitted them out with soft-serve freezers.

Takings per individual van began to decline, and fate decreed that whenever there was a minor heat wave, vans or freezers would break down or the drivers would fail to turn up, preferring no doubt to take the day off and take their family to the seaside.

In order to keep the family business solvent my brothers and I had put our last farthings and savings, even our personal pensions into the business. Our pride could not allow us to see the company go down. We had invested a lot of money in expensive new equipment and new vans, especially during the manufacturing years. At one time we ran a fleet of some twenty vehicles. But the writing was on the wall, under-capitalisation, unfair competition and a series of bad summers caused the bubble to burst. The Knickerbocker Glory years were over, the Great Melt Down was upon us. We had no alternative but to go into voluntary liquidation.

I was to have the bitter experience of facing our creditors at a Hanley office of solicitors. The gloomy event was announced in the London Gazette on 15 February, 1966:

MEETINGS OF CREDITORS G. EMANUELLI & SONS LIMITED: Notice is hereby given pursuant to section 293 of the Companies Act, 1948, that a Meeting of the Creditors of the above-named Company will be held at the offices of Messrs. Peat, Marwick, Mitchell & Co., 17 Albion Street, Hanley in the city of Stoke-on-Trent, on Thursday, the 3rd day of March 1966 at 2.30 o'clock in the afternoon, for the purposes mentioned in sections 294 and 295 of the said Act.— Dated this 10th day of February 1966. Ettore Emanuelli, Director.

And its grim outcome was disclosed on the 8 March 1966:

G. EMANUELLI & SONS LIMITED: At an Extraordinary General Meeting of the above-named Company, duly convened and held at 17 Albion Street, Hanley in the city of Stoke-on-Trent, on the 3rd day of March 1966, the following Extraordinary Resolutions were duly passed: 1. That it has been proved to the satisfaction of the Company that this Company cannot by reason of its liabilities continue its business and that it is advisable that the same should be wound up and that the Company be wound up accordingly. 2. That Roy Geoffrey Lovatt, of 17 Albion Street, Hanley in the city of Stoke-on-Trent, be and he is hereby appointed the Liquidator of the Company for the purposes of such winding-up. E. Emanuelli, Chairman.

I came away utterly humiliated and despondent. This was perhaps the worst day of my life since I had been arrested in June 1940. Had it all been worth while, I wondered. I had lost everything I had worked for since I had sold my father's ice cream at the Opera House in Treherbert in South Wales as a young child, and then again when I had pushed my handcart around the streets of Tunstall as a teenager. Once again I felt lost, isolated and excluded and with a stain on my name.

Now with a large family to support I also began to blame myself for the demise of the business. I felt I had betrayed everything my father and mother had built up in this country since the early 1920s. I had five children and was suddenly hardly in a position to support them let alone to spend large amounts of money on their education. Had I been too ambitious, too proud to even consider that perhaps Emanuel & Sons should not have expanded so rapidly? Should I have perhaps delegated more? Had I lacked business vision?

It was 1966 and I was 45 years old. I was in the middle of my life. My wife was suffering from depression, our family company was bankrupt. I and my brothers were jobless. I had to leave my wonderful home in Biddulph. At a stroke my social life came to a virtual end. No more Ice Cream Alliance dinner dances, no more Knights of Saint Columba meetings in the loft of Biddulph Church. I had no source of income. I seemed to have lost my way and my place in the world. I was just the son of Italian immigrants. Wrongly perhaps, but I felt at the time that I had no particular skills to sell and nowhere to go. All these dark thoughts gathered in my mind, and still do to this day. The opening of Dante's Inferno haunted me:

> *'Nel mezzo del cammin di nostra vita*
> *mi ritrovai per una selva oscura,*
> *chè la diritta via era smarrita.'*

Loosely translated, in the middle of life I had lost my way and had entered a dark wood.

But listening to an inner voice, I realised that self-recrimination was not the answer to my plight. There's nothing else for it Ettore, I thought. 'Stiff upper lip and pull your socks up!'

*A growing family: Anthony in school uniform, Domenic on his mother's arm, Alda with a cuddly toy and Marguerite with a pigtail. Rhyl 1959.
Left: Michael was the highlight of the sixties. He arrived in 1963.*

Anyone for soft ice cream?

CHAPTER 15

The Happy Years

'Yet, after all, the truly efficient labourer will not crowd his day with work, but will saunter to his task, surrounded by a wide halo of ease and leisure, and then do but what he loves best.' Henry David Thoreau, A Week on the Concord and Merrimack Rivers, 1849

It was with sinking heart that I left The Paddock in Biddulph. Fortunately, my father had given me the cash for a deposit on a new house. This naturally softened the blow of unemployment. I found a semi-detached house. Although its dimensions were toy-like compared to The Paddock, it was located in Trentham, a pleasant, leafy suburb of Stoke-on-Trent. There was a spacious garden with two large lawns spread out in front of the house. At the bottom of the back garden, the Trent and Mersey Canal flowed peacefully between grassy banks. Occasionally, gaily painted barges drifted by carrying happy holidaymakers. Birds sang in the copse that bordered the garden on the left. It was small, but idyllic. It was to become 'my little English home.'

I immediately set about seeking a job. Was it, I have often wondered, my guardian angel that directed me just a few months later to apply to the firm of Quickfit and Quartz for employment or was it simply the alliterative name that appealed to me? At any rate, it was in my best suit and with my gold-tipped Parker pen in my breast pocket that I duly attended the firm's offices at Stone for an interview. I must have made some sort of an impression, for I was accepted for the post of Home Sales Correspondent, beginning the following week.

The following Monday morning I reported – with some trepidation – for work at the Quickfit and Quartz offices. I needn't have worried. I was immediately made to feel at home by my fellow office workers.

Little did I realise it on that Monday morning, but I was about to embark on the most happy and contented years of my life. The ice-cream years were now a thing of the past. The bankruptcy of the family business was to turn out to be a blessing in disguise, and I soon found myself more at home in the world than I ever had before.

Joan returned to her nursing position and worked as a sister at the North Staffs Hospital. She was welcomed back with open arms. She had forgotten nothing of the skills she had learned twenty years earlier. She was much loved by her colleagues. This helped her out of the worst of her depression.

To my relief my brothers also quickly found employment, Louis in the computer industry and Aldo in the book trade. Their future was assured. The world looked a lot brighter by the end of the first year after the demise of the family business.

Quickfit and Quartz were manufacturers of high-quality laboratory glassware. Frankly, when I first joined the firm I did not know the difference between a Petri dish and an Erlenmeyer flask, but with the help of my fellow office workers and constant study of the firm's catalogues, I soon became fairly well acquainted with the company's product range.

I quickly became familiar with the functions of a modern office. My job was to correspond by phone and letter with the various customers who came within my Home Sales patch. I learnt to answer their queries, and when I promised to call them back on the telephone I always kept my word even if the news I had to give them was bad. They seemed to appreciate this and within a very short time I had made many friends amongst their ranks.

I remember the elation I felt on Fridays when I marched out through the factory gates. I had done an honest week's work and I was free to enjoy the weekend! Gone was the stress of business worries. I had not had such a feeling of liberation since I had been released from detainment in Brixton Prison back in 1942!

I was soon joining in all the social activities I could at the company. These included inter-departmental quizzes. I became a member of the Quickfit quiz-team and represented the firm on the hospital radio quiz programme. I am reminded of this by the only trophy that I have ever won – the runner's up trophy for the Brain of Quickfit!.

For the next four years I was thoroughly engrossed in Home Sales, steadily adding to my knowledge of glassware. I was indeed very happy during those first years in my new job. Although I had many responsibilities in my work, it was a complete contrast from the worrying and stressful years during the meltdown of the family ice-cream business.

In the seventies I moved to the Export Department, which offered me a higher salary and opened the way to many new and exciting experiences. Coming straight from the Home Sales environment into the export field meant a sharp learning curve. I had to familiarise myself with export terms such as export licences, bills of lading, C.I.F., F.O.B., C.A.D., confirmed and irrevocable letters of credit, and so on. I was to be responsible for the Eastern Bloc countries, including Albania, Bulgaria, East Germany, Poland, Hungary, Romania, Yugoslavia and the Soviet Union.

My team consisted of three persons: myself, a secretary and my boss, Bert Pokora. He was a Polish World War II veteran who had served as a tank commander in the Polish army. Our very efficient secretary was Doreen March. We all got on extremely well together. Unlike 'Home Sales,' there was no telephone contact with prospective customers. All communication was by telex or written request. Very often I would have to contact the foreign embassies in London to discuss prices. Some six months might pass before an order was finally booked. On one occasion I was invited to attend a cocktail party at the Polish Embassy. I mingled with the many guests. There were some suspiciously attractive ladies there, but no untoward advanced were made to me and I rather enjoyed the party. I also went to the Romanian and Hungarian embassies, but I was never invited to any parties there.

Bert made periodical visits to the Eastern Bloc. Before each visit he would say, whilst tapping his nose in a most conspiratorial gesture 'Hector, I shan't be in this afternoon. I have to go to the dentist.' He did this every time. Doreen and I would smile and we wondered whether he was really going to the dentist, after all his teeth seemed in perfectly good order. Or was he being briefed, was he a secret agent? We did wonder.

In the early seventies Bert and I were delegated to represent the company at the International Trade Fair in Poznan. We were to man the firm's stand together with a small team of stand dressers and technicians. We travelled by company car, with our briefcases stuffed full with copies of quotes and brochures. We boarded the ferry from Harwich to Hamburg, where we started our drive through Germany to the border with the German Democratic Republic. The East German border, I recollect, was very intimidating. Barbed wire fences with armed sentries looking down from their watchtowers. I had not seen so much barbed wire since my days in the camps at York, Ascot, Huyton, the Isle of Man and Brixton Prison.

After a long wait and a thorough vehicle search at the border we drove on through GDR territory. I well recollect driving along what appeared to be a military concrete road bordered by tall, dark fir trees on each side. There were no private cars apart from our own. There was a lot of military traffic and police cars, the inmates of which would glance and stare into our car as they overtook. I felt sure that we were being timed and watched in case we took a different route to that set out in our papers.

We eventually reached the Polish border, where the whole procedure was repeated. The drive through Poland was interesting. We passed very few industrial or commercial enterprises. It was clear that this was an agricultural economy with many farmers still using horses for ploughing. It was quite late when we eventually reached Poznan. We checked into the Mercury Hotel, where we were to stay for the coming week. We each had our own room and Bert insisted that – should we have any reason to visit each other – we would not discuss business terms, discounts and so on or policy matters concerning our quotations. He was adamant that our rooms would be bugged. I searched my room, but I could not find any bugs, not of the eavesdropping type that is!

Bert had taught me a few useful phrases in Polish. Polish is not an easy language to learn. I found the lack of vowels a great hindrance. However, I was eventually able to greet visitors to our stand with some degree of cordiality. Bert also introduced me to the Polish custom of greeting ladies with the hand kiss. I must say I got quite adept at this!

During our week on the stand we were kept busy entertaining visiting laboratory technicians and university professors interested in examining our 'thin layer chromatography' apparatus. They showed a great deal of interest in our 3DWS triple water-distillation unit. One professor so much as hinted that it would make an ideal unit for the distillation of illegal vodka!

Now and then, Bert would give me his customary finger-to-nose tapping to let me know that he would be absenting himself from the stand for the afternoon. I don't think that he was visiting the dentist on these occasions, either, but he never divulged what assignations he was keeping.

I was left in charge with an English-speaking student who was very helpful to me in dealing with visitors. I called him Alex. I found his Polish name unpronounceable. Wishing to reward him for his help, I asked him if he would like to come to the hotel for a drink after the stand had closed. 'It would be more than my life was worth!' He whispered. 'I would be reported for consorting with westerners.'

The dining room at the Mercury was always full with exhibitors from the Trade Fair entertaining their prospective customers. The menu consisted of Chicken Kiev with an ample supply of vodka. Every evening Bert and I entertained members of the state's buying organisations, Labimex and Minex. These organisations were responsible for buying laboratory glassware for laboratories and universities. We did all we could to spoil their representatives! We badly wanted an order.

The Fair drew to its close. Alex presented me with a carved walking stick in remembrance of our visit. I still have it today. Bert and I were exhausted after meeting and entertaining so many visitors, demonstrating our various laboratory assemblages, sealing the discussions with the usual tot of vodka! I never really acquired a taste for it, but I always tried to show my appreciation – all in the course of duty.

Bert remained at Poznan for another few days to wrap things up while I flew back to London Heathrow, changing flights in Warsaw .

A little later back at the office in Stone a telex message arrived bringing the good news that Labimex had accepted our quotation and that a large order was on its way. The order duly arrived. It was worth a quarter of a million dollars. This was the largest single order ever received by the company to date and it was thumbs up all round as I walked through the factory floor. The Directors and Management treated Bert and myself to a sherry party and for a time we were the blue-eyed boys!

It was the custom at Quickfit and Quartz to fly the flag of the country of whichever visiting VIP was calling on us. Driving into our car park one morning, I noticed that the Japanese flag was flying over the office. Ah well, I thought, that did not concern me. Japan was not part of my remit. I was very surprised, therefore, that half way through the morning the managing director sent for me. He introduced a certain Mr Moto from Japan, who represented a company the name of which I admit escapes me now.

'Mr Moto says he would very much like to visit the Marks and Spencer's store in Stafford. I thought that you would like to take him there. I believe he would like to purchase some presents for his wife.' Like most Japanese businessmen, Mr. Moto was very polite. He gave me a courteous bow and I returned the gesture.

We left the office and made our way towards Stafford and the Marks and Spencer store. He was very affable, and thanked me profusely for escorting him. He said that he would like to buy his wife some jumpers. He said he had heard that Marks and Spencer's clothing was of the highest quality. I conducted him to the ladies' wear department. To my utter amazement Mr Moto said to me 'My wife is exactly your size. Would you please model these jumpers for me?' I was, to say the least, taken aback, and extremely embarrassed as I tried on one ladies jumper after the next in full view of the many lady customers in the department. I was getting some very strange looks. Mr Moto eventually chose six jumpers and we made our way to the cash point. I was on tenterhooks and as we made our way out of the department. I made sure we bypassed the lingerie section. That would have been going too far!

My position at Quickfit and Quartz left me a lot of time for other activities, something I had never known before in life, except – ironically – when I was imprisoned during the war. I joined the firm's Sports and Social Club and in particular the Drama Group. In 1979, this became known as Stone Little Theatre. We produced shows for the employees and also for the general public. I was happy painting the scenery and working as Front-of-House Manager. With what artistic talents I possessed I designed and made models of the sets for approval by the director. All of these sets were well received, I'm glad to say.

Among the shows we produced I can recall the play 'Here we Come Gathering,' a comedy by Phillip King and Anthony Armstrong. We also put on 'Ten Little Indians' by Agatha Christie and 'Babes in the Wood' as a New Year pantomime. When we staged 'A Funny Thing Happened to Me on the Way to the Forum' Frankie Howard actually sent us a signed photograph wishing the cast all the best for our production of this well-known and loved comedy. We followed this with 'The Ghost Train' by Arnold Ridley. I was especially pleased with my design for this set.

Over the years we produced many more plays, comedies and pantomimes. I can recall the pantomime 'Aladdin,' for which I based my design for the set and backdrop on the Willow pattern. This, too, was a great success. I have always loved live-theatre ever since I sold ice cream as a little boy in the Opera House at Treherbert, and those days spent painting and erecting sets for the various productions gave me much pleasure.

My job also left me time to develop a new interest: rambling! At weekends and during my holidays I would venture out, sometimes alone but often with colleagues. This new interest really took off in 1983 when I went into early retirement.

I joined the Ramblers Association and soon became involved in helping to arrange the walking programme for the Stoke-Newcastle Group. I made many friends and was soon leading walks and week-long walking holidays in the Brecon Beacons, the Lake District, and the Yorkshire Dales. Over the years we walked on the Isle of Wight, where my good friends Sylvia and Peter Prescott led many and interesting walks. We walked the 'Heart of England Way' and took a coach trip to Stratford-upon-Avon, where I had gone to school as a little Italian boy with a big Welsh accent.

We also spent an enjoyable week on the Isle of Man, where I was able to take our group to the scene of my detainment at Peel, and where I showed my friends the exit to an escape tunnel that was built by some of the prisoners. I must stress, however, that I never took part in the digging of the tunnel, which was a closely-guarded secret among the hard-liners involved in the escape.

I took great pleasure in originating and organising the City of Stoke-on-Trent Parks and Heritage Walk. This is a linear walk of some 14 miles. Canal towpaths and greenways link up the City Parks of the Five Towns, allowing walkers to avoid the roadways. This was first walked by the then Mayor and Mayoress of the city in 1991 when we set off from Longton Park. I have taken many groups since then on this Heritage Walk.

In 1996 thirteen of us set off for a weeks walking holiday on the west coast of Scotland, Ardnamurchan. This is still remembered today by all those that took part. Keith Storr, who sadly is no longer with us, led the walks with great expertise and much hilarity. It was on the slopes of the heather clad hills that I lost my dentures, much to the amusement of the group. It was at the Strontian Hotel where we met for our evening dinners that we let our hair down. We entertained the locals each evening and it was on the last night of our stay that they all acclaimed 'Will ye no come back again?'

My rambling holidays gradually became increasingly international, and Italy was naturally a favoured destination. In September 1998 twenty of us set off for a two-week holiday in the Alto Adige area of northern Italy. We stayed at the Lady Maria Hotel in Fondo in the valley of the Non. Splendid walking country, especially in the Dolomites. A couple of years later, a thirteen-strong party from the Stoke-and-Newcastle Group enjoyed a September holiday in the spa town of Fiuggi, set in the Aurunci mountain area near Rome. We visited Rome and Monte Cassino. Over the years we have walked the Tuscan shores of Viareggio, the Lago d'Iseo, Bad Aussee in Austria. We have seen Samos in Greece, Ladis in Austria, the hills around Rome, and the Douro valley in Portugal. I could write volumes about each of these walking holidays, but space and time dictate otherwise.

But in 2007, to crown it all, I took a group of some twenty of my English friends to Liguria in northern Italy for a walking holiday. From there I took them over the hills to Bardi, where a welcome committee headed by Signora Ester Zanelli, the President of the local magazine 'Famiglia Bardigiana,' spent the whole day showing us around. We had lunch in the Bue Rosso, where my mother had worked as a waitress all those years ago. The Bue Rosso has a wonderful dining room with panorama windows overlooking the valley. As I chatted with my English friends and let my gaze wander down the river Ceno to the bluish horizon I felt completely at home.

The best job I ever had! On the telephone in the Export Department at Quickfit & Quartz in Stone. The work was interesting, and at the week-ends I was able to do but what I loved best – rambling, designing stage sets, gardening, painting.

Quickfit and Quartz in 1972. Celebrating the record-breaking order from Poland.

One of my many hobbies: designing stage-sets. Here I am on the set I designed for 'The Ghost Train' for Stone Little Theatre in 1981.

The canal that flows past my back garden in Trentham. In summer it is a paradise of sunlight, shade and birdsong. This is the little English home where I have spent so many happy years.

Rambling has given me so much pleasure. Here I am with fellow ramblers in Cannock Chase in 2005.

CHAPTER 16

Epilogue

Knickerbocker Glory

I have many bitter recollections of the first half of my life. I suffered from a feeling that I did not belong. As a little boy, I stuttered and yearned for the magic Italian valley that economic circumstances had obliged my parents to leave to seek work in South Wales. When I had learned to love Wales, I was uprooted to live in England – a country that was foreign to me and which treated me with disdain. During my early years in Tunstall my family's dire financial straits forced me into menial employment, putting an end to my formal education when I was still just a boy. I had hardly put down roots in the Potteries, which I have learned to love as my home, when I was arrested on the suspicion that I was a member of a fascist fifth-column plotting sabotage and the overthrow of democracy. My hopes of pursuing a creative rather than a business career were thwarted by my parents' unspoken assumption that I should work for the 'family business.' Much hard work and endeavour restored my fortunes, but only briefly. In the middle of life I was declared bankrupt and left without employment, an outsider again.

Despite all this, however, I am convinced that throughout my life I have had the protection of a guardian angel who has always picked me up every time I have fallen. He picked me up again in 1966 when the family business was forced to close down. As if by magic, he found me employment that amused me and which gave me enough time to pursue all those interests I had hankered after in my younger years. From that moment onwards, my life has been like that wonderful and supreme ice-cream confection that Emanuel & Sons used to serve at the Wonder Bar and the Cafe Continental in Tunstall all those years ago: the Knickerbocker Glory. This masterpiece of the art of ice-cream making is always served, or at least it should always be served, in a tall elegant glass with a long-stemmed silver spoon. It consists of a multi-layered arrangement of various flavours of ice cream, sauces, fruits and chopped nuts, the whole topped with a cloud of fresh whipped cream and crowned with a maraschino cherry. Every layer is good.

As I dip my spoon into the whipped-cream topping of my imaginary Knickerbocker Glory my memory takes me back fifty five years. Our five-year-old daughter Marguerite is performing in a school ballet at the Queen's theatre in Burslem. As the youngest performer in her group she drew much applause, but loving her as we did we realised that she was not destined for the Royal Ballet. After attending St. Dominic's High School she took up a career as a children's nurse at the Booth Hall Hospital in Manchester. She now lives in Saudi Arabia with her two daughters and grandchildren where she teaches part time and is studying Arabic.

Rich dark chocolate sauce with chopped walnuts and zabaglione have always been my favourite and as I relish this layer in my imagination my mind goes back to the year 1968. I had decided to take my fifteen-year-old daughter Alda Maria Silvia and my ten-your-old son Dominic on a motoring holiday to Italy. This was the first time that I had driven abroad and we set off in our not-too-reliable Morris Eleven Hundred saloon. We had a few punctures en route. We stopped at Rheims in France and then again in Lausanne. Then, having bravely scaled the Alps, our little Morris faltered on the Italian motorway, the result of an over-heated engine, which was in turn the result of a leaking radiator. Our rescuer was a handsome young white-uniformed Fiat rescue-service operative. After many admiring glances in Alda's direction he soon got us going on our way to the Adriatic coast and Rimini and Cattolica. Here my paternal and protective instincts took over as Alda in her mini-skirt was attracting so many admiring glances from the locals. We had many adventures with the Morris Eleven Hundred, driving through hill-top towns when the fuel gauge always seemed to read zero, with no petrol station for miles, but we always seemed to make it. Alda sported herself in her bikini on the beach while Domenic tried to bury me in the sand.

   I have now an amalgam of vanilla ice cream, fresh peaches and raspberry sauce. For some inescapable reason my mind goes back to the year 1973, when I was on holiday in Scotland, Loch Linnie, near Fort William. I was determined to attempt Ben Nevis and it did not need much encouragement to get my young son Michael, then ten years of age, to come with me. It was a glorious morning. Rucksack packed with ample provisions and bottles of water, we made an early start. Climbing steadily with frequent stops to admire the ever-changing views we made good progress. Passing isolated snow gullies as the air got cooler and looking forward with anticipation to our final attempt on the summit. Deep snow all around, at last we had made it. In the still glorious sunshine we ate our picnic lunch and played around in the snow admiring the distant views all around us, greeting fellow climbers as they too reached the summit. We made a very leisurely descent, sad in a way to have to leave the top of Britain's highest mountain. We were both tired, but on reaching our base Michael turned to me and exclaimed 'Thanks Dad, that was great, something I'll never forget!'

   My spoon reaches the layer of pistachio and vanilla ice cream, and my mind wanders back to a time some ten years ago, walking in Tuscany whilst on holiday with my son Anthony and his wife Margit. A pair of beautifully ornamented gates, partly open and with an inviting glimpse of a garden, cedar trees, marble statuary and well-trimmed lawns, lure us into what we believed was a public park. After looking around for a few minutes, we are approached by a gentleman, who we assume to be the gardener. Anthony in his fluent Italian engages him in conversation. It appears that we have accidentally walked into his private domain. Anthony makes our apologies. But the gentleman insists on conducting us around his beautiful estate, explaining that his family had lived here for centuries. He was the perfect host and may well have stepped out of a renaissance painting. Before we left he told us that he was count of something or the other, I'm afraid my memory fails me. I remember Margit laughing that evening as we recounted our story and she served us one of her marvellous Italian dinners.

These are the Knickerbocker Glory memories from the sweeter second half of my life and though these sweet years now appear to be racing by at an ever increasing rate, I am not yet quite ready to give up the ghost. I still enjoy walking, though the walks tend to be shorter. I still enjoy my visits to the theatre, the opera and concerts. I'm still in love with Bardi and all things Italian. Gardening still also takes up a lot of my time and each year I try to make improvements to my garden. I still look forward to holidays in Italy.

As you will have read, it was in 1943 that I picked my English Rose. It was Student Nurse Joan Hulse who cared for me as I convalesced in the recovery-ward at the Haywood Hospital in Burslem. In 2008 we celebrated our Diamond Wedding, with a card from Her Majesty the Queen to prove it! Sadly, Joan passed away in November 2009. Her last words to me were 'Hector, I always loved you.' She was and still is my English Rose! I would have been so happy if she had been able to read this book.

As I ski down the final slopes of my life I am sure my guardian angel will be waiting again to catch and embrace me as I reach the end of the run, and Joan will be standing at his side.

Joan and I reminiscing.

*Author **Hector Emanuelli** was born in 1920 in the small mining town of Abercarn in South Wales. As a boy he hawked ice cream for his father 'refreshment houses' in the Rhondda Valley. His education at Pentre Sec was cut short when his parents moved to England, where he worked as a lodge-boy in a pot bank in the Potteries and sold ice cream on the streets of Tunstall. Interned as a potential fifth-columnist during the war, he was released in 1942. In the post-war years he and his brothers went on to build their parents' family ice-cream business into a prosperous enterprise. He retired in 1983 and since then has dedicated his time to his many interests: Italian literature and art, the history of the English landscape, the theatre and stage-set design, opera, rambling and gardening. He has lived in Trentham, Stoke-on-Trent, for over forty years.*